SAM SHEPARD

The Late Henry Moss
Eyes for Consuela
When the World Was Green

Sam Shepard is the Pulitzer Prize–winning author of more than forty-five plays as well as the story collections *Great Dream of Heaven* and *Cruising Paradise* and two collections of prose pieces, *Motel Chronicles* and *Hawk Moon*. As an actor he has appeared in more than twenty-five films, and he received an Oscar nomination in 1984 for his performance in *The Right Stuff*. His screenplay for *Paris, Texas* won the Grand Jury Prize at the 1984 Cannes Film Festival, and he wrote and directed the film *Far North* in 1988. Shepard's plays, eleven of which have won Obie Awards, include *Buried Child, Simpatico, Curse of the Starving Class, True West, Fool for Love,* and *A Lie of the Mind,* which won a New York Drama Desk Award. A member of the American Academy of Arts and Letters, Shepard received the Gold Medal for Drama from the Academy in 1992, and in 1994 he was inducted into the Theatre Hall of Fame. He lives in Minnesota.

The Late Henry Moss

Eyes for Consuela

When the World Was Green

SAM SHEPARD

The Late Henry Moss

Eyes for Consuela

When the World Was Green

THREE PLAYS

Vintage Books

A DIVISION OF RANDOM HOUSE, INC.

NEW YORK

A VINTAGE BOOKS ORIGINAL, NOVEMBER 2002

Library of Congress Cataloging-in-Publication Data
Shepard, Sam, 1943–
[Plays. Selections]
The late Henry Moss ; Eyes for Consuela ; When the world
was green : three plays / Sam Shepard.
p. cm.
ISBN 987-1-4000-3079-8
I. Title: Eyes for Consuela.   II. Title: When the world was green.
III. Title.
PS3569.H394 L37   2002
812'.54–dc21   2002072086

Book design by Rebecca Aidlin

www.vintagebooks.com

Printed in the United States of America
10 9 8 7 6 5 4 3

CONTENTS

The Late Henry Moss

The Late Henry Moss was first produced by the Magic Theatre (Larry Eilenberg, Artistic Director), San Francisco, on November 7, 2000, with the following cast:

HENRY MOSS	James Gammon
CONCHALLA	Sheila Tousey
EARL MOSS	Nick Nolte
RAY MOSS	Sean Penn
ESTEBAN	Cheech Marin
TAXI DRIVER	Woody Harrelson
FUNERAL ATTENDANT 1	Rod Gnapp
FUNERAL ATTENDANT 2	Dennis Ludlow

Directed by Sam Shepard
Designed by Andy Stacklin
Costumes by Christine Dougherty
Lighting by Anne Militello
Composer and music archivist T Bone Burnett
Choreography by Peter Pucci
Production stage managed by Michael Svenkel

It was produced in New York by Signature Theatre Company (James Houghton, Founding Artistic Director; Bruce E. Whitacre, Managing Director) on September 23, 2001, with the following cast:

HENRY MOSS	Guy Boyd
CONCHALLA	Sheila Tousey
EARL MOSS	Arliss Howard
RAY MOSS	Ethan Hawke
ESTEBAN	Jose Perez
TAXI DRIVER	Clark Middleton
FUNERAL ATTENDANT 1	Michael Aronov
FUNERAL ATTENDANT 2	Tim Michael

Directed by Joseph Chaikin
Designed by Christine Jones
Costumes by Teresa Snider-Stein
Lighting by Michael Chybowski
Original music and sound by David Van Tieghem
and Jill B.C. Du Boff
Choreography by Peter Pucci
Fight direction by B. H. Barry
Production stage managed by Michael McGoff

Prelude to Act One: (Drunken Rumba)

Lights go to black on set. In the dark, very sultry Mexican rumba music comes up. A white spotlight hits the couple of Henry Moss and Conchalla wrapped in a tight embrace, cheek to cheek. They are amazingly drunk and yet synchronized in tight, fluid coordination with only the occasional stumble and foot crunch to give them away. They begin extreme down left on the apron in front of the set and careen their way across the stage, doing a couple twirls and deep waist bends along the way. Their cheeks stay pressed together the whole time, and they seem oblivious to the world. The dance is brief and somewhat shocking. They disappear off right. Spotlight goes to black, then lights ease up on set to begin Act One.

Act One:

Scene: *Night. A run-down adobe dwelling on the outskirts of Bernalillo, New Mexico. The roof is open; just bare, rough-plastered walls. A mesquite door with black iron hinges in stage right wall. A deep-silled window up right. A single cotlike bed set horizontally into a small alcove, center of upstage wall with a small barred window directly above it, like a jail cell. There is a blue curtain on a rod in front of the bed that can be opened or closed by hand and sometimes mechanically. The curtain is open for now, revealing the corpse of Henry Moss, a man in his late sixties. He lies face up on the bed with the crown of his head toward stage right. A heavy Mexican blanket in yellow and red designs covers him from the forehead* *down to his ankles. Over the blanket a white sheet has been spread smoothly. Only the top of Henry's head and his bare feet are revealed. Nothing is seen of his face. There is an old-style bathtub with claw feet upstage left of the bed. A sink, gas stove and small refrigerator are set against upstage wall; all very run-down and dirty. Extreme downstage left of center is a simple round Formica table with two metal S-shaped chairs set across from each other; one upstage right, the other downstage left. Earl Moss, Henry's oldest son, sits in the downstage chair with his back partially to audience, thumbing through an old photo album of Henry's, studying the pictures. Ray Moss, Earl's younger brother, stands upstage of the table, facing audience and idly going through an old red tool chest of Henry's placed on the table in front of him. A bottle of bourbon sits in the center of table with two plastic cups. An ashtray; cigarettes. Nothing else. Long pause after lights come up as Earl thumbs through album. Ray fiddles with tools.*

EARL: [*Thumbing through album.*] Well, you know me, Ray—I was never one to live in the past. That never was my deal. You know—You remember how I was.

RAY: Yeah. Yeah, right. I remember.

EARL: But, these days now—I don't know. Something like this— Outta the blue. [*He nods toward Henry's corpse.*] Maybe it's age or something.

RAY: Age?

EARL: Yeah.

RAY: Whose age?

EARL: Mine.

RAY: Oh. I thought you meant his.

EARL: No—me. Gettin' older. You know. I mean at eighteen, nineteen, my mind was going in a whole different direction. You remember how I was. [*He suddenly sings.*] "Gonna tie my pecker to a tree, to a tree. Gonna tie my pecker to a tree." You remember that? [*Pause. Ray just stares at him.*]

EARL: Well, do ya?

RAY: I thought that was him. I remember him singing that.

EARL: That was me!

RAY: Oh.

EARL: 1956, '57? When was that?

RAY: What?

EARL: When I used to come home singing that.

RAY: I don't know. Musta been later.

EARL: Not that much later. Couldn't a been. Ripple wine and Mexican Benzedrine! Those were high times, Ray! High old times. [*Pause.*]

RAY: I remember you leaving. That's all I remember.

EARL: [*Looking up at Ray.*] What? When?

RAY: When you first left. When the big blowout happened.

EARL: Big blowout?

RAY: You know what I'm talkin' about. [*Pause. Earl stares at him.*]

EARL: Ooh—that. Way back.

RAY: Yeah.

EARL: Way, way back.

RAY: That's still very vivid with me. Like it happened yesterday.

EARL: [*Going back to album.*] You shouldn't let that stuff haunt you, Ray.

RAY: I remember the windows exploding.

EARL: Exploding?

RAY: Blown out. Glass everywhere.

EARL: Ooh—yeah. That was *him* [*Gestures to Henry*], not me. That was him doing that.

RAY: Yeah. Him.

EARL: You're getting me mixed up with him.

RAY: No I'm not. I know it was him.

EARL: Well, don't get me mixed up with him.

RAY: I'm not. I know it was him.

EARL: Good. [*Pause. He thumbs through album.*] *He* was the one breaking windows. Not me.

RAY: I know that. [*Pause.*] What brought it on exactly? That was never very clear to me.

EARL: Oh, come on, Ray—

RAY: What?

EARL: You mean after all this time—after all these years—you still don't know?

RAY: No. I never knew.

EARL: She locked him out of the house. You knew that, didn't you?

RAY: Um—I don't know. Yeah, I guess.

EARL: Set him right off. Went into one of his famous "Wild Turkey" storms. You knew all about that.

RAY: I remember it like a war or something. An invasion.

EARL: Yeah, well things get embellished over the years. You were a kid.

RAY: So were you.

EARL: Yeah, but there was a certain—maturity about me. I was coming into my own back then.

RAY: Explosions. Screaming. Smoke. The telephone.

EARL: Explosions? There weren't any explosions, Ray.

RAY: People running. You were one of them.

EARL: What?

RAY: Running.

EARL: I never ran!

RAY: Mom was running.

EARL: He had her trapped in the kitchen! Under the sink! How could she run? Huh? How could she possibly run? You've really got this screwed up, Ray. You oughta get it straightened out, you know. It's time you got it straight. It's no good carrying the wrong pictures around with you the rest of your life. They're liable to get more and more warped as time goes on. Pretty soon you'll start to forget how it really was.

RAY: You ran. I watched you.

EARL: I never ever ran!

RAY: You climbed into that '51 Chevy and took off. That was the last I saw of you for seven years. Things like that you don't forget. They mark time. For *me* they do.

EARL: [*Returns to album.*] Yeah, well—I never ran. I'm not a runner. Never have been. [*Pause.*]

RAY: Seven years. Thought I'd never see you again. I thought about you all that time but I bet I never once crossed your mind. Never once.

EARL: That's not true.

RAY: Maybe once.

EARL: Once or twice.

RAY: Once, maybe.

EARL: I sent you something every Christmas. Most every Christmas, I did.

RAY: Yeah.

EARL: Socks. T-shirts. Rubbers. I sent you Camels once.

RAY: Tokens. Tokens of guilt.

EARL: [*Looking up.*] Guilt? Look—buddy boy, I had a lot on my mind back then.

RAY: Yeah.

EARL: I was heading somewhere. [*Long pause. Earl goes back to album. Ray fiddles with tools.*]

RAY: What should we do with his tools?

EARL: You want 'em? You might as well keep 'em.

RAY: I don't work with my hands anymore.

EARL: Oh? Since when?

RAY: I don't know. It just faded.

EARL: That's a shame, Ray. You were good with your hands. You used to be under a car all day long.

RAY: What car?

EARL: Some car. I don't know what car. Some car or other.

RAY: I never had a car.

EARL: Well, whose car was it, then, you were always working under?

RAY: It was his car.

EARL: Okay.

RAY: It wasn't my car.

EARL: Fine.

RAY: Well, it wasn't. I never had a car. You were the one with the car.

EARL: All right! It was *his* car, it wasn't your car! Who gives a flying fuck whose car it was! I just seem to remember, Ray, that you always liked working on cars and I thought you might like to have the tools in case you wanted to pursue that. That's all. Simple as that. [*Long pause. Earl goes back to album. Ray handles tools.*]

RAY: [*Handling tools.*] Looks like they're all pretty cheap anyway. Taiwan steel. Swap meet stuff.

EARL: You oughta keep 'em, Ray. For his sake you oughta keep 'em.

RAY: For his sake?

EARL: Yeah.

RAY: He's dead.

EARL: I know he's dead.

RAY: So why should he care?

EARL: He won't care, Ray.

RAY: So it'd be for *my* sake, not his sake.

EARL: Yeah. For your sake. You never can tell when the urge might come up again.

RAY: What urge?

EARL: To work with your hands! That urge! The urge to be useful again! [*Pause.*]

RAY: [*Looking at tools.*] They're not worth diddly.

EARL: That's not really the point, is it, Ray. I mean nothing he's got is worth diddly. Not like we're inheriting a legacy here.

RAY: Ratchet's pretty nice. [*Ray picks up a very large ratchet wrench and fits a socket onto it.*]

EARL: Why don't you keep that, then? He'd like that, Ray.

RAY: Keep the ratchet?

EARL: Yeah. Keep the ratchet. It's a nice one, right?

RAY: A single big-ass ratchet? What am I gonna do with a single ratchet?

EARL: Work on your Buick! I don't know.

RAY: I don't have a Buick.

EARL: Goddamnit, Ray!

RAY: Well, I don't. You want me to say I have a Buick just so you can feel good about giving me these crummy tools? They're not your tools anyway. You don't own the tools.

EARL: I know I don't own the tools!

RAY: They're his tools.

EARL: I know that.

RAY: They're not yours to give away.

EARL: They're not yours either!

RAY: They're nobody's tools! [*Ray slams the wrench back into toolbox. Long pause. Earl goes back to album. Ray turns upstage and stares at Henry's corpse, then turns back to Earl.*]

RAY: Well, don't you think it's about time we notified someone? We can't just sit around here. Who're you supposed to call first? The cops?

EARL: The cops? What're you thinking about?

RAY: Who, then? The mortician? The chamber of commerce? Who?

EARL: [*Back on album.*] I'm not ready yet. [*Pause.*]

RAY: *You're* not ready?

EARL: No. I'm not.

RAY: Well, how long are we gonna wait?

EARL: [*Looks up.*] What's the rush? Huh? I'd like to spend a little time with him if you don't mind.

RAY: Time?

EARL: Yeah, time. Before he's rushed off and processed into the funeral business. Before they apply the makeup and formaldehyde and dress him up in his air force khakis.

RAY: Well, how much time do you need, Earl?

EARL: I'll let you know.

RAY: Haven't you been sitting here with him for a long time already?

EARL: I'll let you know, Ray.

RAY: What've you been doing just sitting here with him all this time?

EARL: Nothing.

RAY: Have you been talking to him, Earl?

EARL: He's dead.

RAY: Yeah, but when you're alone like this—just sitting here—just the two of you—You can start to make stuff up.

EARL: What stuff?

RAY: Stuff in your head. You can start—imagining things.

EARL: Like what?

RAY: Well, like for instance—you could imagine that he's still alive; he can still hear you—Maybe it's even better that way.

EARL: What way?

RAY: Imagining. I mean that might be even better than if he were actually alive because now you can really tell him things. You can tell him all kinds of things that you couldn't tell him before because now he's dead and you're imagining him to be alive and there's nothing he can do about it but listen.

EARL: I wasn't talking to him, all right! I wasn't imagining anything! I was just sitting here! Alone. With him. Just sitting here in the dark. Alone. [*Pause. Ray turns upstage and starts to move slowly toward Henry's body.*]

RAY: We can't just bury him ourselves, huh? Just dig a hole and do it ourselves? That's illegal, isn't it?

EARL: Yeah, every death has to be reported these days. Unless you kill somebody.

RAY: We could report it *after* we bury him.

EARL: They'd just dig him back up.

RAY: I mean that's what you'd do with a dog—

EARL: What?

RAY: Just dig a hole and bury him.

EARL: Yeah.

RAY: So how come you can't do that with a father? [*Moves in closer to Henry's corpse. Earl pours himself a drink, smokes and keeps thumbing through album.*]

EARL: I don't know. I don't know the answer to that, Ray. I don't know why that is. Nobody cares about a dog. I guess that's it.

RAY: [*Getting very close to Henry.*] Nobody cares about a dog.

EARL: Well, they don't.

RAY: You mean outside the dog's little circle of friends? His little family.

EARL: Yeah, nobody cares. [*Ray reaches out to touch Henry's corpse. Earl stands suddenly.*]

EARL: Don't touch him! [*Long pause. Ray stares at Earl.*]

RAY: What?

EARL: Just don't touch him.

RAY: Why is that, Earl?

EARL: Just—don't. It's not a good idea. [*Pause. Ray looks at corpse, then back at Earl.*]

RAY: Am I gonna catch something—some disease?

EARL: Just—get away from him.

RAY: Have *you* touched him?

EARL: No.

RAY: It's not gonna hurt anything, is it? [*Ray goes to touch the corpse again, but Earl makes a strong move toward him.*]

EARL: Don't touch him, Ray! [*Ray backs off.*]

RAY: What're you so jumpy about?

EARL: I'm not jumpy.

RAY: Are you superstitious or something?

EARL: I just don't think it's a good idea to touch him.

RAY: Afraid he might come back to life?

EARL: That's pretty funny. [*Pause.*]

RAY: He's starting to stink, Earl. I think he's starting to stink.

EARL: I can't smell it.

RAY: Yeah, well, you've been with him too long. You've grown insensitive to it.

EARL: Insensitive. *Me*, insensitive?

RAY: Yeah. There's a stink in here. There's definitely a stink and you can't smell it.

EARL: That's right.

RAY: How long's it take before things really start to rot. You know—

EARL: How should I know? I'm no expert on death. [*Earl returns to table, sits and goes back to album.*]

RAY: I mean really bad—turning to maggots.

EARL: We're not gonna wait *that* long, for Christ's sake! Just try to relax a little, Ray. All right? Just relax. Feel honored that we have this small time alone with him. Try to treasure it. [*Pause.*]

RAY: Honored?

EARL: That's right, *honored*. Somebody else could've discovered him first. Anybody. A total stranger. The taxi driver or that crazy chick—what's her name—or—anybody. They'd have called the cops right off the bat. The mortuary boys would've been here already with a body bag and hauled him off. And there we'd be. We'd be the last ones notified. No privacy. All kinds of questions. Forms to fill out. We'd never have had two seconds with him by ourselves. [*Pause.*]

RAY: What taxi driver?

EARL: What?

RAY: What taxicab driver?

EARL: The taxicab driver. The guy who picked him up and took him fishing. The guy who brought him back.

RAY: Same guy?

EARL: Yeah. Same guy. I told you that. I told you all about that on the phone.

RAY: Well, if he picked him up and brought him back, how would he have discovered him dead? He would've had to die in the taxi.

EARL: I was just saying that as an example!

RAY: It's not a good one.

EARL: I was just using the taxicab driver as an example of any-one! How it could've been anyone other than us who found him first!

RAY: Who did find him first?

EARL: *I* found him first! I told you that. You never listen.

RAY: And you just decided to sit here with him.

EARL: Sit here until you got here. I figured it was my duty.

RAY: Your duty?

EARL: That's right, my duty.

RAY: "Duty and honor, duty and honor." Doo-wah, doo-wah, doo-wah duty.

EARL: Go fuck yourself, Ray. [*Pause. Earl goes through album.*]

RAY: So, who's this crazy chick?

EARL: What?

RAY: This crazy chick you mentioned as one of the possible candidates who might've found him first?

EARL: His girlfriend.

RAY: His girlfriend?

EARL: Yeah. Whatever her name was—"Conchita" or something.

RAY: "Conchita"?

EARL: Something like that.

RAY: "Conchita Banana"?

EARL: Don't get cute. Have some respect for the dead. I went through all this stuff with you before on the phone. Don't you ever listen to anything?

RAY: I was in shock.

EARL: Well, snap out of it! [*Pause. Ray slowly circles table around Earl's back, then returns to the chair across from Earl and slowly sits. He pours himself a drink.*]

RAY: [*As he crosses behind Earl.*] I'm still in shock. I wasn't expecting to be in shock but I guess that's the thing about shock.

EARL: What?

RAY: It's unexpected. You don't see it coming. You just find yourself in the grips of it. You do the best you can.

EARL: [*Focused on album.*] Why don't we take a walk or something, Ray? This New Mexican air might just do us some good.

RAY: [*Seated with drink.*] I know this is going to probably irritate you a whole lot, Earl, but would you mind going back through the whole story for me one more time?

EARL: What story?

RAY: The stuff this guy—what's his name? The neighbor?

EARL: Esteban?

RAY: Yeah—Esteban. That's it. The stuff this guy, Esteban, told you on the phone when he called you in New York. *Before* you found Dad dead. What happened just before? I'm a little lost here. [*Pause. Earl pushes the album away and with a long exhale, stares at his brother.*]

EARL: What's the matter with you?

RAY: Me? Nothing. Nothing's the matter with me. I'm his son. You're his son. I've got a right to know, as much as you do. We're both blood.

EARL: I told you everything already, once!

RAY: Yeah—Yeah, you did. But there's some stuff that doesn't make sense.

EARL: What stuff!

RAY: There's all these—all these people you mentioned. It's just too—stupid! It's stupid that he died like this! Out here in the middle of nowhere with no—contact. No contact whatsoever!

EARL: That's the way he *lived*! He lived with no contact. Why shouldn't he die the same way? [*Pause. Ray drops his head slowly and stares at the table. Earl stares at him.*]

EARL: All right—All right. Once more and that's it. I can't keep going through this, Ray. It's not something I enjoy.

RAY: Why would you enjoy it?

EARL: I *don't* enjoy it! That's what I'm saying.

RAY: Then why even bring it up.

EARL: Goddamnit, Ray, you are such a little piss-ant.

RAY: That may be. That may well be. A "piss-ant." I'd just like to hear the story again, Earl. The whole story. [*Pause. Earl stares at him, then begins.*]

EARL: I got the phone call. Collect. Esteban says he's worried about the old man.

RAY: This was a week ago or something?

EARL: That's right. A week ago. About a week. Before I called you. Now listen up! Try to pay attention this time.

RAY: I'm all ears.

EARL: He's worried—Esteban. He's the neighbor. He says Dad got some money in the mail. Henry's cashed a check that came in and he's walking around with this cash burning a hole in his pocket.

RAY: Where'd the check come from?

EARL: Who knows. GI check or something. Government pension. I guess he was always getting these checks and going on binges. He's buying booze with it. He gets a haircut. He hitchhikes down to the shopping center. He wanders around downtown, drunk. Then he wanders down to the gas station and buys a fishing license.

RAY: Drunk?

EARL: Yeah, drunk. What else? Then he hitchhikes back out here and calls a taxi from Albuquerque. Taxi picks him up and he takes off for a day and goes fishing. He comes back that night with this Indian chick.

RAY: The crazy one?

EARL: The crazy one. [*Ray nods for Earl to continue.*]

EARL: So, the taxi waits for him and the woman. Esteban sees the cab outside, so he comes over with some soup.

RAY: Soup?

EARL: That's right. Soup, Ray. That's exactly right. Esteban was always bringing Henry soup or chili or some damn thing. Trying to sober him up. Esteban says the woman's in the bathtub, giggling. She's half-naked and drunker than skunk.

24

Esteban drinks with them but Dad won't eat the soup. They
have a big argument about the soup and Henry kicks him
out. Esteban stays outside by his trailer and keeps watching
the house. He sees Henry come out with the Indian woman
wrapped in a blanket. She's still giggling. They pile into the
taxi and take off. That was the last he saw of him.

RAY: So when you got here, after this phone call from this
neighbor—I mean, I'm trying to put all this together—How
many days did it take you to get here?

EARL: You mean after the phone call?

RAY: Yeah.

EARL: I don't know—three or four.

RAY: Three or four days?

EARL: Yeah. I guess. I don't know.

RAY: It took you three or four days after you hear that he's in
trouble?

EARL: I had some business to take care of!

RAY: Business? What kinda business, Earl?

EARL: Packaging! I got a packaging business now. We make
boxes.

RAY: So after your "packaging business" you fly down here,
walk in the door and find Henry dead in his bed? Is that it?

EARL: Yeah. That's it! Just like that. Just how he is right there. I haven't touched him. He was laying there stroked out on his back just like he is right now. All I did was cover him up. [*Long awkward pause. Ray gets up and goes to window. He stares out. Earl watches him.*]

EARL: So—How's the family? [*Ray doesn't move from window. Keeps his back to Earl.*]

RAY: What family?

EARL: Your family. Out west.

RAY: I don't have a family.

EARL: Oh—I thought you got married and uh—Somewhere I heard you got married.

RAY: I never had a family.

EARL: Oh—[*Ray turns toward Earl but stays near window.*]

RAY: How's *your* family?

EARL: I don't have one either. You know that.

RAY: How am I supposed to know that?

EARL: Have I ever mentioned a family to you?

RAY: No—but I thought maybe—

EARL: Maybe what?

RAY: Maybe you had a secret family.

EARL: A secret family?

RAY: Yeah. [*Pause.*] No?

EARL: No.

RAY: That's too bad, Earl.

EARL: If I had a secret family, why would I tell you about it?

RAY: Because I'm your buddy, Earl. I'm your little buddy. You can tell me all your secrets. [*Pause.*]

EARL: Look, Ray—There wasn't much either one of us could do about this. You know that. He was on his way out. Been that way for a long time. Pickled. Pissing blood. The shakes. Blackouts. Hallucinations. There was all kind of signs.

RAY: Signs.

EARL: Yeah. He stopped eating, for one thing. [*Pause. Ray crosses over to refrigerator and opens it. It's completely empty except for a small jar of jalapeño peppers. Ray takes the jar out, closes fridge, crosses to table and sets jar on it.*]

RAY: Jalapeños.

EARL: Can't stay alive on peppers and hooch. [*Ray opens jar, sits at table and starts eating the peppers, chasing them down with bourbon.*]

RAY: How do we get ahold of this taxicab driver?

EARL: What?

RAY: The taxicab driver who took Dad fishing.

EARL: You got me. You'd have to find out what company it was first.

RAY: Well, Esteban would know that, wouldn't he? The friendly neighbor? He saw the cab.

EARL: Well, yeah, but—good luck finding the driver.

RAY: Shouldn't be that hard. They keep records. Every car has a number. Every driver. It's the law. They log in, they log out.

EARL: What's the taxicab driver gonna tell you?

RAY: I dunno. Something. Maybe he saw something. [*Earl slides the album toward him, showing him an old photo of their father as a boy. Ray doesn't look at it: just keeps chewing on jalapeños.*]

EARL: Look at this. Here he is with his dog, Gyp. Look at that. "1931" it says. 1931. So, he's how old there? How old would he have been?

RAY: Maybe he'd know how to find that Indian woman.

EARL: [*Still with album photo.*] Well, let's see—that's thirty—no— fifty-seven years ago? So—fifty-seven—he would've been— he would've been twelve years old there. Twelve years old! Imagine that!

RAY: Maybe she saw something.

EARL: So who's president then? Hoover? Or was it FDR?

RAY: Maybe she can tell us what happened.

EARL: Look at that. There he is. No idea what's in store for him. Just a kid standing in a wheat field with his dog. [*Ray slams the jar of jalapeños on the table and stands.*]

RAY: Why did he suddenly take it into his head to go fishing, Earl! Why is that? You don't take a taxicab to go fishing! Why is he suddenly up in the mountains with an Indian chick fishing! It doesn't make any sense! I woulda gone fishing with him! Why didn't he call *me* to go fishing! I love to fish! Why didn't he call *me*! [*Pause. Earl just stares at him.*]

EARL: You were far away, Ray. [*Pause. Silence. The door swings open wide and Esteban, a small, skinny Mexican man in his fifties, very neatly dressed in khaki pants, light pink shirt with dark blue tie and shiny black shoes, is standing in doorway holding a large green bowl of steaming soup with both hands. He smiles broadly at the brothers and just stays there in open doorway. Earl stands quickly from table and moves toward him.*]

EARL: Esteban! Come on in.

ESTEBAN: Is Mr. Henry here? I saw the light on.

EARL: Come in, Esteban. Good to see you. [*Esteban begins to cross, very slowly, toward table, keeping his eyes glued to bowl of soup, careful not to spill a drop. It takes him a very long time to reach his destination.*]

ESTEBAN: [*As he crosses slowly.*] I brought Mr. Henry his soup. He sometimes will eat. Sometimes not. Depends on his mood. How you catch him. I was very worried this time. He just disappear like that.

EARL: [*Closing door.*] Esteban, this is my brother, Ray. He just— came in from California.

ESTEBAN: [*Keeps moving, eyes fixed on bowl.*] Glad to meet you, Mr. Ray. *Mucho gusto.* [*Ray nods, stays where he is by window. Earl crosses to table, ahead of Esteban, and moves the album to make room for the soup's arrival. Esteban keeps smiling and inching slowly across the room with soup.*]

ESTEBAN: [*Crossing slowly.*] I put vegetables and chorizo in there for his blood. Habaneros. I know how the blood can get from liquor. I was a drinking man, myself. Many years. Oh, yes. They couldn't stop me. Nobody. Many people weep for me but I could not hear them. Bells rang in all the chapels but I was deaf.

EARL: Do you want me to take that for you, Esteban?

ESTEBAN: No, no, no—I can manage, Mr. Earl. Many bowls I have balanced across the road for Henry. Many years of practice. The timing I know by now. The soup it cools down just right from my trailer to his door. Henry no like it too hot. One time he burn himself so bad he almost kill me. It was funny but he almost did. I could see the murder in his eye. Real murder. The pain had make him crazy. I tell him, is such a little pain, Mr. Henry. Don't kill me for such a little pain as this. Wait for a bigger pain to kill me! [*He laughs, then stops himself when he sees he might spill the soup.*] But he was drunk—so he no laugh. He no laugh with me.

RAY: Who is this?

EARL: Ésteban. [*Pronounced incorrectly with accent on first syllable.*] The neighbor.

ESTEBAN: [*Pronounced correctly.*] Estéban.

EARL: [*Repeats the mispronunciation.*] Ésteban. [*Esteban finally reaches the table and sets the soup down very carefully. He smiles and sighs with relief, then pulls a soup spoon and napkin out of his back pocket and sets them neatly beside the bowl. He pulls a salt shaker out of his back pocket and places it in front of the soup. Pause. Earl looks at Ray, then back to Esteban, who is smiling broadly.*]

ESTEBAN: So—is Mr. Henry home now from fishing? I was very glad to see the light here. Very, very happy. I was afraid he might just—vanish.

EARL: He's—He's sleeping, Esteban. Worn out, I guess.

ESTEBAN: [*Looks toward Henry's corpse.*] Ooh. [*Lowers his voice to a whisper.*] That is good. He need that. He need that after fishing. [*Esteban tiptoes over to Henry's bed and looks at corpse.*]

EARL: Don't uh—Don't disturb him now, Esteban.

ESTEBAN: [*Keeping distance from Henry.*] Oh, no.

RAY: Yeah. Don't touch him, whatever you do. My brother's liable to go ape-shit. [*Ray crosses to table, sits; pours a drink.*]

ESTEBAN: [*Whispering, looking at Henry.*] No, he need sleep. He need plenty of that. More than soup, he need sleep.

EARL: Yeah, he could use some sleep.

ESTEBAN: I bet you—[*He giggles.*] I bet you that big crazy woman wore him out. You know, Mr. Earl? That Indio woman. [*Laughs.*] She is so—you know—[*Cups his hands under his chest.*]—Robusto! No? Very strong woman. Right, Mr. Earl? A lot of woman for Henry.

EARL: Yeah—I don't know.

ESTEBAN: He have fun with her I bet. [*Giggles and sways.*] She bend his back like a willow tree. She fuck him silly! [*Esteban bursts out laughing and jumping up and down.*]

EARL: Don't do that—Don't wake him up. Okay, Esteban? [*Esteban quiets down and goes back to whispering. Ray watches from the table, somewhat perplexed.*]

ESTEBAN: Oh, no. No, no, no. He need his sleep. That is good for Henry. I was so worried when I saw he have that money. So much money. That is why I call you, Mr. Earl.

EARL: I'm glad you did, Esteban.

ESTEBAN: So much money in his hand. It is no good when a man is fighting his weakness. Too much money. [*Esteban sneaks up closer to bed and stares at corpse.*]

ESTEBAN: He sleep very peaceful. Very still.

EARL: Yeah—He's exhausted.

ESTEBAN: I can barely hear him breathe. Maybe the blanket's covering his nose too much. [*Esteban moves as though to lift the blanket away from Henry's face. Earl leaps at him.*]

EARL: Don't touch him!!!!! [*Esteban leaps back away from Henry and stands there in shock. Pause.*]

RAY: [*To Esteban.*] I tried to warn you about that.

EARL: I'm sorry, Esteban—I'm just uh—I'm a little worn out myself. [*Esteban stays frozen where he is, staring at Earl. Earl moves toward Esteban but Esteban backs up from him.*]

EARL: Why don't you uh—Have a seat or something. It's okay, Esteban. Everything's fine. [*Pause. Esteban keeps staring at Earl.*]

RAY: Esteban—you live right across the road here, is that right? You're the neighbor?

ESTEBAN: [*Turning toward Ray.*] Yes, sir.

RAY: How long have you lived over there, Esteban?

ESTEBAN: Thirty years.

RAY: Thirty years.

ESTEBAN: *Más o menos.*

RAY: Thirty years in a trailer.

ESTEBAN: Yes, sir, Mr. Ray.

RAY: So, you've known my father for a good long time, then.

ESTEBAN: Yes, sir. Ever since he move here from California. When he have that bad time.

RAY: Which bad time was that, Esteban?

ESTEBAN: When he think the world was trying to eat him.

RAY: What?

ESTEBAN: When he think—He was doomed, he said.

RAY: He said that?

33

ESTEBAN: Yes, sir. I have times like that myself but Henry never believe me. He think he was the only one.

RAY: Doomed?

ESTEBAN: Yes, sir.

RAY: Can it with the "sir" shit, all right! I'm not your "sir."

EARL: Take it easy, Ray.

RAY: Well, what does he think this is, the military or something? I don't need that "sir" stuff.

EARL: He's just being polite, you idiot! It's a rare thing these days.

RAY: Polite?

EARL: Politeness. It's okay, Esteban. [*Pause.*]

RAY: You want a drink, Esteban? Me and my brother have been kinda gettin' into Henry's bottle here a little bit.

ESTEBAN: Oh, no, no, Mr. Ray. Thank you, no. I no touch liquor no more. No more for me. [*Giggles.*] Is finished. Too many beautiful women have leave me. Now—when I need them most, they are gone. And I am sober. Is funny, no?

RAY: Yeah. That is pretty funny. [*Pause.*] So, you don't drink at all? Is that the story, Esteban?

ESTEBAN: No, sir. No more for me.

RAY: Well, my brother was just telling me you knocked one back now and then with the old man.

ESTEBAN: [*To Earl.*] Oh, no, Mr. Earl! I pretend with Henry. Only pretend. He never notice. *Muy borracho!* [*Turns back to Ray.*] Long as I make the motion, you know. [*He mimes taking a drink.*] Tilt the glass; bend the elbow—That is all he cares. Just the motion. He like the company, your father. He like the human—smell.

RAY: So, you mean—that night, when the taxi came to pick him up, you were just *pretending* to drink with him? You were— [*Mimes drink.*] just pretending?

ESTEBAN: Taxi? Oh, yes. Pretending. *Sí.* Only pretend. [*Pause. Ray looks at Earl, then back to Esteban.*]

RAY: And uh—Henry just kinda went along with that, I guess, huh? He was so happy to be in your company—So starved for human companionship.

ESTEBAN: [*Laughs.*] He was very drunk, Mr. Ray. Very, very drunk. Like a mad dog.

RAY: And this—woman—"Conchita" or whatever her name was— she was very drunk too? Very, very drunk?

ESTEBAN: Conchita? [*Pause. Esteban turns to Earl. Earl shrugs.*]

EARL: I don't know. He just doesn't get the picture, Esteban. I been trying to explain it to him—

ESTEBAN: "Conchita"? [*Laughs.*] "Conchita," no! You mean Con- challa. Conchalla Lupina! No, "Conchita."

RAY: Conchalla Lupina?

ESTEBAN: [*Laughing.*] *Sí Eso.*

RAY: [*To Earl.*] Conchalla Lupina? Sounds like an opera singer.

EARL: Does kinda, doesn't it. Conchalla Lupina.

ESTEBAN: Conchalla! She is—*magnífica!* You would not believe this woman, Mr. Ray!

RAY: Is that a fact.

ESTEBAN: She is—She is—How do you say it? Your father will tell you. She has—a big reputation down here in Bernalillo. [*Laughs.*]

RAY: Is that right? How'd she come by that? [*Esteban stops himself. He and Earl exchange looks. Pause. Ray stares at them.*]

RAY: What's going on between you two? Something's going on here.

EARL: Nothing's going on.

RAY: Something's going on. What's the deal with this woman?

ESTEBAN: Oh, Mr. Ray—Conchalla is very mysterious woman. With a woman like this, believe me, a man could die in her arms and thank the saints! He could pray for no better way to leave this suffering world.

RAY: Yeah, I'd like to meet her.

ESTEBAN: They say she has done men in like that. The lucky ones. Can you imagine something like that?

RAY: Something like what, Esteban?

ESTEBAN: Oh, you know, Mr. Ray. You know—[*Esteban begins to gyrate his pelvis and go into frantic laughter, holding his stomach, then he suddenly stops. Ray stares at him.*]

ESTEBAN: Oh, I am sorry, Mr. Ray—I get—when I think of her I—If you saw her you would know. She would burn a hole right through your heart! Right here! [*Stabs his chest with his fingers.*] Right through the center of your soul! Right there! [*Esteban pokes his finger hard into Ray's chest, then quickly backs away.*]

ESTEBAN: Oh—I am sorry, sir. [*Short pause, then Ray leaps out of chair and grabs Esteban by the collar.*]

RAY: [*Shaking Esteban.*] What'd I tell you about that "sir" shit! Huh? What'd I fuckin' tell you! [*Ray shoves Esteban backward. Esteban trips back and falls to the floor.*]

EARL: [*Going to Esteban.*] Hey! What is the matter with you, Ray? You gone nuts or something?

RAY: I warned him! I told him about that "sir" stuff. I don't like the implication.

EARL: [*Helping Esteban to his feet, brushing him off.*] What implication? What're you talking about?

RAY: I haven't done anything to earn that kind of respect from him. That's something you say to someone you respect. He

doesn't know me from Adam. How does he know I'm somebody he should respect?

EARL: Well, he knows now, doesn't he?

RAY: Yeah. Yeah! Maybe he'll think twice before he goes around
calling strangers "sir." Who does he think he is, calling me
"sir"? [*Earl moves to Ray, holding his finger up.*]

EARL: Look, pal—

RAY: Go ahead, Earl. Poke me in the chest. I need to get poked
again. Real hard. Right here! [*Ray pokes his own chest, daring
Earl. Pause. Earl glares at him as Esteban stands by.*]

RAY: Come on, Earl. It's been a long time, hasn't it? [*Pause with
the brothers staring each other down as Esteban watches. Earl
backs down and turns away from Ray.*]

EARL: Look—Let's just relax here, all right? How 'bout we just
relax?

RAY: I am relaxed. "Pal." [*Earl moves to table, sits and pours himself a drink. Esteban keeps staring at Ray.*]

EARL: [*At table.*] No need to get all worked up over nothing.
Things are hard enough. You gotta be careful at a time like
this. I mean—How 'bout we just have a—have a drink.

RAY: He doesn't drink, remember? He *pretends* to drink. He's a
pretender.

EARL: Back off, Ray! What kind of a bug have you got up your
ass anyway? Huh? The man comes over here with *soup*. He

comes over here just as polite and neighborly as he can be and you jump all over him like a cold sweat! What is the matter with you?

RAY: Tell him to stop staring at me.

EARL: You've terrified him is what you've done.

RAY: Tell him to stop staring at me.

EARL: Come on, Esteban—[*Moves toward Esteban.*] Look—I apologize for my brother's behavior—

RAY: Don't apologize for me! I don't need you to apologize for my behavior! Tell him to stop staring at me. [*Earl escorts Esteban back to table and sits him down.*]

EARL: Everything's fine. Don't pay any attention to him. He—flies off the handle like this—I don't know. He—it'll be all right. Everything's fine. [*Earl sits Esteban down, then sits in the other chair. Pause.*]

RAY: [*Mimicking Earl.*] "Everything's fine." [*Pause. Ray stares at them. Esteban sticks his finger in the soup.*]

EARL: Everything's fine, Esteban.

RAY: Stop saying that! Stop saying that over and over again like some lame prayer! Everything's *not* fine! Everything's the opposite of "fine"! "Fine" is when your heart soars! When you're in love or something. That's when things are "fine." Right, Esteban? "Fine" is—[*Ray suddenly stops. Long pause. Earl and Esteban stare at him.*]

RAY: I wanna know about this woman.

EARL: What woman?

RAY: This woman—This mysterious woman; "Conchalla," "Conchita," whatever her name is.

ESTEBAN: "Conchita." [*Esteban starts giggling uncontrollably. Short pause.*]

RAY: Shut up!! You shut up!! [*Esteban stops abruptly. Short pause.*]

RAY: Who is she, Earl?

EARL: His girlfriend. Henry's girlfriend.

RAY: Well, see now that—just confuses the hell outta me. I never even knew Henry had a girlfriend.

EARL: I told you he had a girlfriend.

RAY: You told me jack shit, Earl.

EARL: I told you on the phone.

RAY: How long's he had this "girlfriend"? Where'd he meet her?

EARL: I don't know where he met her. [*Pause. Earl won't answer.*]

RAY: Where'd he meet her, Esteban?

ESTEBAN: In jail.

RAY: In jail. That's cute. [*He turns to Earl.*]

EARL: I never met the woman, myself.

RAY: *You* never met her but Esteban here knows all about her evidently.

EARL: I heard he had a girlfriend but I never actually laid eyes on her.

ESTEBAN: They meet in jail.

RAY: What do they have, a coeducational drunk tank down here in Bernalillo?

ESTEBAN: They meet in jail.

RAY: That where you met her too?

EARL: Don't get personal.

RAY: Well, this is kind of a personal thing here, Earl. Girlfriends and jail. This is something different than a photograph from 1931. This is something actual here.

EARL: The man's a neighbor!

RAY: Yeah, right. Come here, neighbor! I wanna show you something. [*Ray grabs Esteban by the back of the neck, hauls him out of the chair and starts taking him toward Henry's corpse. Earl leaps up.*]

EARL: What're you doing! [*Earl grabs ahold of Esteban's arm and pulls against Ray.*]

RAY: Come here. Now take a look at this.

EARL: Ray! [*Ray manages to swing Esteban upstage at the head of the bed with Earl still holding on to him. Ray is downstage of the bed, back to audience. He whips the sheet and blanket back, revealing Henry's face to Esteban but blocking it from view of the audience. Esteban stares at the corpse.*]

RAY: Go ahead—Touch his face, Esteban! This is Henry. "Mr. Henry"! The man you've been bringing soup to for all these years. [*Ray grabs Esteban's hand and pushes it down on the face of the corpse. Earl tries to pull Esteban away but it's too late.*]

RAY: [*Holding Esteban's hand down on corpse.*] You feel how cold that is? Like ice! Like stone in a river. Does that look like a man who's ever gonna eat another bowl of soup? [*Ray releases Esteban's hand and spreads the sheet and blanket back over the corpse, covering the head completely. Esteban just stands there in shock, trembling. Earl moves slowly back toward table. Pause.*]

RAY: So—

EARL: [*Moving toward table.*] You better get outta here, Ray.

RAY: I just got here, Earl.

EARL: There's a certain—kind of cruelty to you, isn't there? I never realized that before.

RAY: Yeah, I get mean as a snake when I don't see the whole picture.

EARL: [*Referring to Esteban.*] You had no call to be doing that to him.

RAY: What're we gonna do? Pretend?

EARL: You come waltzing in here—No idea—No concept what-soever.

RAY: Concept? [*Earl sits at table. Esteban begins to softly weep upstage.*]

EARL: Yeah. Yeah, that's right. No concept that there might be repercussions. That there might be consequences—serious consequences.

RAY: [*Moving toward Earl.*] Have you lost your tiny mind out here, Earl? Is that what's happened to you? Sitting here all alone with dead Daddy for days on end. Something went on here! Didn't it, Earl? Something I'm not being let in on!

EARL: Nothing went on!

RAY: "Nothing went on." "Everything's fine." [*Moves in closer to Earl.*] Henry was tough as an old boot! You know that. He could kill two pints and a six-pack in one sitting and never skip a beat! Now you want me to believe he takes off on a two-day binge with some Indian chippie and drops dead overnight? Is that what you're telling me?

EARL: [*Smashes down on table.*] It was an accumulating illness!! He was a fuckin' alcoholic, Ray! [*Long pause. Just the sound of Esteban softly weeping.*]

RAY: [*To Esteban.*] Stop that goddamn whimpering! [*Esteban stops.*] You weren't related to him, were you? [*Esteban shakes his head, stands there trembling by Henry's bed.*]

RAY: Then what're you carrying on about? I'm his *son*! You don't see me whimpering, do you? [*Esteban shakes his head.*]

RAY: I've got every right to be whimpering but you don't see me doing that.

EARL: Ah, Ray, give it up.

RAY: [*Turning on Earl.*] Or you! What about you? I suppose you think you've got some sort of private thing going—some kind of special link to the corpse or something. You're in deep communion here with old Henry. [*Pause.*] Old dead Henry. [*Pause.*]

EARL: What'd you ever come out here for, Ray? Why'd you even bother?

RAY: I just couldn't believe it, I guess.

EARL: You thought he'd live forever? Is that it?

RAY: No. I just thought—

EARL: What?

RAY: Maybe I'd see him one more time. Alive.

EARL: Yeah. You thought maybe you'd get to the bottom of something—clear things up? Make some big reconciliation.

RAY: I don't need any reconciliation! I don't need it with you either!

EARL: Good. That's good, Ray—because, guess what? It'll never happen. He's gone now. [*Earl moves away from Ray to Esteban. He puts his arm around Esteban's shoulder and pats him, then starts leading him toward door.*]

RAY: What're you doing?

EARL: We're gonna go down and make that phone call, Ray. Down to the Sonic there.

RAY: What phone call? The meat-wagon boys? So—your little period of mourning has suddenly come to an end?

EARL: Let it go, Ray! Give it up! Go on back to wherever you came from. [*Pause.*]

RAY: No—No, I'm not gonna give it up, Earl. You know why? Because I'm your witness. I'm your little brother. I saw you, Earl! I saw the whole thing.

EARL: You saw shit.

RAY: I saw you! [*Earl takes Esteban toward door.*]

EARL: Come on, Esteban.

RAY: I saw you run!! [*Earl suddenly whirls around and attacks Ray. He overpowers him and sends him crashing across stage into refrigerator. Ray hits the floor. Earl crosses to him and kicks Ray in the stomach. Ray collapses. Esteban stays by door, watching. Pause as Earl straightens out his coat, then turns back to Esteban. Ray stays on floor.*]

EARL: I'm sorry about all this, Esteban. I truly am. I hate this kind of thing, myself. Family stuff. [*Earl moves toward Esteban, then stops about halfway. He looks back at Ray, then to Esteban.*]

EARL: I had no idea my brother was so screwed up in the head like this. I mean I knew he had some problems but I thought he'd pulled himself back together. Otherwise I'd never have called him. Anyhow—We better go make that call. [*Earl goes to door and opens it for Esteban. Esteban exits, then Earl turns back to Ray.*]

EARL: [*To Ray on floor.*] Well—At least this'll give you a chance to spend a little time alone with Henry, Ray. Maybe that's what you need. Did me a world of good. [*Earl exits, closes door behind him. Pause. Ray stares at door, then hauls himself to his feet, holding his ribs. He stares at Henry's corpse, then crosses to bed and stops with his back to audience. Pause as he stares down at corpse; then, with a quick jerk, he draws the curtain closed in front of the bed. Short pause, then lights fade quickly to black.*]

Prelude to Act Two: (Drunken Rumba)

Lights go to black. A new, more spirited mariachi piece comes up to volume. White spotlight hits Henry and Conchalla on the opposite side of stage this time (extreme downright). They are still amazingly drunk and in the same tight embrace. Again they dance across the apron, doing some variations, and disappear off left. Spotlight out; lights up on set to begin Act Two.

Act Two

Scene: *Day. Same set. The sound of rubber gloves snapping in the dark; labored breathing. Lights come up fast on two funeral attendants dressed in gray suits, flesh-colored rubber gloves, dark glasses and white gauze masks covering nose and mouth. They are struggling to place Henry's corpse inside a black canvas body bag. They are having a great deal of difficulty getting the body to fit into the bag. They work nervously, under the constant scrutiny of Ray, who sits in the downstage chair facing them and sipping on his drink. Taxi, a cab driver from Albuquerque, stands upstage of the table, facing audience. He is drinking from a bottle of Tiger Rose and fiddling with the tools in Henry's toolbox, which is still on the table. The photo album lies open on the table where Earl left it. Ray stays completely focused on the funeral attendants as Taxi rambles on.*

TAXI: [*To Ray.*] Hey, look—for a hundred bucks and a bottle of Tiger Rose—are you kidding? This is gravy! This is a day off

47

for me. I'll just regard it as that. A whole free day, thanks to you. Whatever your name is. I didn't catch the name—[*Taxi toasts Ray with the bottle but Ray ignores him. Attendants continue struggling with body in background.*]

TAXI: I mean, all the dispatcher told me is, some guy from Bernalillo wanted to talk to me. That's all the information I got. [*Pause.*] Oh, well—I was on the verge of quitting anyhow, if you wanna know the truth. Company sucks. All they care about is the damn meter. Human interest is not number one on their list. Far as they're concerned they'd just a soon have a damn robot drive the cars. Cut their insurance in half. It's coming to that. I guarandamnteeya. Computerized robot taxis. You won't even see a human being behind the wheel anymore. I'm not lyin'. [*Pause. Attendants keep working, making some progress, trying to zip the bag shut. Ray keeps watching them intently. Taxi drinks and picks up the large ratchet out of the toolbox, the same ratchet Ray was handling in Act One. He starts fooling with it as he talks, causing the ratchet to make a rhythmic clicking.*]

TAXI: Oh, well—Thank God I'm self-sufficient. I could head on out to Norman, Oklahoma, and get me a job easy. Plenty a cabs out there. College town too. Plenty a babes. A whole slam a "Miss Oklahomas" have come outta Norman, lemme tell ya. I ain't lyin'. You wouldn't believe the types. Legs up to here. Asses like hard cantaloupes. Some gorgeous babes in that country. No question. I could head on out there and be in high cotton. [*Pause. Taxi keeps clicking the ratchet. Ray keeps staring at attendants as they work.*]

TAXI: Nice ratchet.

RAY: Don't mess with that.

TAXI: What?

RAY: I said, don't mess with that.

TAXI: Oh. Sorry. [*Taxi puts ratchet back in toolbox; takes another swig.*]

RAY: That doesn't belong to you.

TAXI: No—I know. I was just uh—admiring it, that's all. [*Pause. Attendants keep working.*]

TAXI: Were these your daddy's tools?

RAY: They're mine.

TAXI: Oh. Pretty nice. Cheap but nice. [*Taxi idly shifts to the album and starts leafing through it.*]

RAY: [*Focused on attendants.*] Don't mess with that either.

TAXI: Okay. Sorry. Just—Just lookin' that's all.

RAY: Well, don't look. It's none of your business.

TAXI: Right. [*Pause.*] Well—Like I was saying about uh—Norman.

RAY: Who's Norman?

TAXI: No—I mean, uh—Norman, Oklahoma. You know—Like I was saying before about Norman, Oklahoma—

RAY: What about it?

TAXI: Well—I mean, that's what I was saying—I can go on out there and if the taxi deal doesn't work out I can always get in on the midnight pizza delivery thing. You know—Late-night stuff. I've heard all about it, believe you me. Two, three in the morning sometimes, you can get a delivery call. Take a pineapple combo over to some dormitory, for instance. Well—you know who orders a pineapple combo, don't ya? [*Pause. Ray doesn't look at him; keeps watching attendants.*]

RAY: What?

TAXI: I said, you know who usually orders a pineapple combo, don't ya? Girls! That's who always orders those pineapple combos. Girls mostly. So there you are in the perfect setup! Standing there on the front stoop, ringing the bell with red pizza juice dripping down your elbow. And who comes to the door but the goddamn Miss America Contest! [*Henry's body, now encased in the bag, suddenly crashes to the floor as the attendants lose their grip. Ray stands abruptly. Everyone freezes. Pause.*]

RAY: That's my father you just dropped. That's not a piece of luggage or a sack of feed! That's my father. Get out. Get outta here. [*Attendants exit.*]

TAXI: They don't care. They're just hauling stiffs. They've seen it a thousand times. A corpse is a corpse. Might as well be road kill to them.

RAY: Shut up.

TAXI: You need some help with that? [*Ray motions "no." Goes to door and calls back the attendants.*]

RAY: You guys come back. Both of you come back in here. [*Attendants reenter and lift Henry's body again, struggling with the weight as Ray slowly closes in on them. Taxi stays where he is.*] You aren't the type of creeps who make sick jokes behind other people's backs are you? Because if you are I'll find out about it and I'll seek vengeance on your heads. [*Pause.*] Now get outta here. [*The attendants hustle the corpse out the door and disappear. Ray stays in open doorway looking offstage, after them. Taxi stays at the table with album.*]

TAXI: [*Laughing, still going through album.*] That's good! That's good! "I'll seek vengeance on your heads!" That's a good one. Where'd you come up with that? I'll have to remember that. I can use that. That has a kinda—old-fashioned ring to it. You know, like—King Arthur or something? Remember him? [*Ray closes door and turns to Taxi. Pause. They stare at each other.*]

RAY: What'd I tell you about that album?

TAXI: What? [*He quickly looks back at album.*] Oh—[*He shuts album.*] Sorry. I forgot. [*Pause. Ray moves to Henry's empty bed. He stares at bed, then smoothes the blanket and sheet. He draws the curtain closed in front of bed and just stands there staring at curtain with his back to Taxi. Pause.*]

TAXI: [*Stays by table.*] Well—Anyhow, I appreciate the hundred bucks and the Tiger Rose. I surely do. Came as a complete surprise to me when the dispatcher gave me the message. Not that I don't deserve it. [*Laughs.*] I deserve every bit of it. You better believe it! [*Pause. Ray doesn't move, just keeps staring at bed with his back to Taxi.*]

TAXI: How'd you track me down, anyhow? That's a big mystery. I couldn't figure that one out. I mean it's been almost a week ago I was out here. Least a week, wasn't it? I lose track. [*Pause. Ray doesn't move. Silence.*]

TAXI: Well, anyhow, I suppose this is a hard time for you, huh? I mean, I don't mind answering any questions you might have. You said you had some questions. Not that I could tell you much—[*Pause. Ray turns to him and stares, then moves downstage to table and sits; pours himself a drink. Taxi slowly pulls out a chair, as though to sit down at the table.*]

RAY: [*Cold.*] Don't sit down at this table. [*Taxi freezes, then stands and pushes chair back in place. Pause.*]

RAY: I don't know you well enough for you to be sitting at this table.

TAXI: Right—Uh—Sorry. I was thinking—maybe if I sat at the table—we could uh—we could get to know each other—a little—maybe. You know—break the ice. [*Laughs.*]

RAY: What makes you think I want to get to know you? I didn't pay you to come all the way out here so I could get to know you. What do you think you are?

TAXI: Me? Well—I'm—

RAY: Go over and stand by the door.

TAXI: What? [*Pause. Taxi looks toward door, then back to Ray, but doesn't move.*]

RAY: [*Pointing to door.*] Over there. [*Taxi looks to door again, then back to Ray.*]

TAXI: Now, you mean?

RAY: Yeah. Now. When you're a stranger in somebody's house, you don't automatically assume you can sit down at their table and fool around aimlessly with their father's possessions.

TAXI: I thought they were yours. You told me—

RAY: Go over and stand by the door!! [*Taxi looks at door again, then back to Ray. Pause, then he crosses to door, taking his bottle with him, and stands there. He stares at Ray.*]

TAXI: Right here?

RAY: A little to your right. [*Taxi adjusts his position slightly.*]

TAXI: How's this?

RAY: That's good. Now stay right there. Okay?

TAXI: Okay. [*Takes a drink from his bottle.*] Sure. You bet.

RAY: Don't move from that spot.

TAXI: Okay.

RAY: See if you can manage that. Now, just for a minute, try to avoid thinking of yourself as anything special. All right? Anything out of the ordinary. You're nothing. Just like me. An empty nothing. A couple of nothings whose lives have never amounted to anything and never will. Do you think you can go along with this?

TAXI: Well, I don't know. I mean—it's not exactly the way I was raised. My uncle used to—

RAY: I'm not interested in the way you were raised, or your uncle.

TAXI: Right.

RAY: I'm not interested in Norman, Oklahoma, or "babes" or pizza juice dripping down your arm or your employment problems either.

TAXI: Right.

RAY: I'm only interested in one thing.

TAXI: [*Pause.*] What's that?

RAY: What happened that night you showed up here in your cab to take my father out to go fishing? What exactly happened? [*Pause.*]

TAXI: Oh. Well—I don't know. Nothin' special. I mean, I got the call. You know, it was kinda unusual but—[*Taxi starts to move toward Ray.*]

RAY: Just *stay* by the door! [*Taxi freezes, then returns to his spot by the door. Pause. He takes another drink from his bottle.*]

TAXI: Right here?

RAY: A little to your left. [*Taxi adjusts his position.*]

RAY: That's fine. Now—You were saying—It was unusual?

TAXI: Yeah.

RAY: Kind of unusual but not all *that* unusual.

TAXI: [*Stays put.*] No, right. I mean—we get calls now and then from folks way out in the boondocks like this. This is big country—Lotta ground between places. Folks need a ride. Stranded folks. I mean, I remember as a kid we grew up a hundred and twenty miles from the nearest drive-in.

RAY: Don't get off the subject. [*Pause.*]

TAXI: What?

RAY: Your mind is wandering. Don't allow it to do that.

TAXI: Oh—Yeah—Well—like I was saying—all I do is drive 'em to the nearest movie. Forty, fifty miles maybe sometimes. Just to see Clint Eastwood.

RAY: You arrived here at the house! Right? I don't care how long it took you to get here. You arrived. Now, what was going on here at the house when you arrived?

TAXI: Here?

RAY: Yeah. That's right. Here.

TAXI: Oh. Well—nothing really. I mean—I remember knocking. I remember this feeling like—maybe I was at the wrong house or something.

RAY: Why was that? [*Lights slowly shift. A glowing amber light comes up on the curtain in front of Henry's bed. At the same time the lights on the rest of the stage dim to a pale moonlit glow.*]

TAXI: Well, I mean—there wasn't any answer at the door. I kept knocking and—[*Taxi moves slowly toward the curtain and the bed as Ray turns slowly in his chair until he's directly facing the audience. Ray stays in this position, looking directly out at audience through the entire flashback.*]

TAXI: [*As he crosses to curtain in front of bed.*] I could hear something from inside so I knew there was somebody in here. I kept knocking but all I heard was this moaning like—this weeping. I didn't know what to make of it. Door was open so—I just let myself in. And there he was—lying on his side in bed there. Sobbing like—[*The curtain opens slowly on its own, revealing the living Henry, lying on his belly, softly weeping. Taxi approaches him.*]

TAXI: [*To Henry.*] Mr. Moss? [*Pause.*] Mr. Moss? [*Henry suddenly sits up on the edge of the bed with a jerk and stares blankly at Taxi. He stops weeping. Pause. He gets up fast and snatches the bottle of Tiger Rose away from Taxi, then crosses to the door, staggering slightly.*]

HENRY: [*Crossing to door.*] The hell you doin' with my bottle! The fuck is this? Time is it, anyway? [*Henry opens the door, looks out, then slams it shut. He turns to Taxi and stares at him.*]

TAXI: Did you—call a cab, Mr. Moss?

HENRY: A what?

TAXI: A taxi. From Albuquerque? "Verde Cabs"?

HENRY: Taxi? The fuck is this? A taxi from Albuquerque?

TAXI: Somebody called a cab.

HENRY: Somebody?

TAXI: Somebody must have.

HENRY: What if they did? Maybe they did, maybe they didn't. What's the big deal? [*Henry crosses to table and sits in upstage chair, ignoring Ray, as though Ray didn't exist. Henry drinks from Taxi's bottle.*]

HENRY: [*Looking at bottle.*] The fuck is this junk? [*Pushes bottle on table.*] Where'd this come from?

TAXI: I'm the taxi.

HENRY: What?

TAXI: I'm the taxi from Albuquerque.

HENRY: [*Laughs.*] *You're* the taxi? That's something! You look like a damn taxi. You got that yellow stripe down your back. [*He grabs bottle back and drinks, then gags on it.*] What the hell is this stuff anyhow?

TAXI: Tiger Rose.

HENRY: Stuff stinks! [*Pushes bottle away again.*] That's not my stuff. Where the hell's *my* stuff? [*Henry stands and starts wandering around looking for his bottle.*]

TAXI: Did you wanna go somewhere, Mr. Moss? Did you want me to take you somewhere?

HENRY: [*Searching.*] I had a bottle here. You didn't walk off with my damn bottle did ya?

TAXI: No, sir, I just got here.

HENRY: Well, somebody's got my bottle!

TAXI: Mr. Moss, did you need me to take you somewhere? That's what I'm here for. I'm here to take you wherever you want to go.

HENRY: [*Stops, looks at Taxi.*] You're here to take me?

TAXI: That's right.

HENRY: Where do I wanna go?

TAXI: Well—That's what I'm here to find out—I mean—

HENRY: Where could it be that I wanna go?

TAXI: I have no idea, sir.

HENRY: What the hell happened to that bottle! [*Henry starts searching for bottle again.*]

TAXI: Maybe that was it, huh? Maybe you needed me to take you to get a bottle?

HENRY: That's what you think. That's probably what you think! Do I look that desperate to you?

TAXI: No, sir.

HENRY: You lyin' sack a doggy doo-doo.

TAXI: I'm going to have to go, Mr. Moss. [*Taxi makes a move to leave. Henry stops him.*]

HENRY: Just a second, just a second, just a second! Just hold on here. You're the taxi, right?

TAXI: That's right. Yeah.

HENRY: And you've got a mission. Is that it? You were called to come here?

TAXI: Yes, sir.

HENRY: So somebody musta called you out here. Is that correct?

TAXI: Yeah. That's correct.

HENRY: And you think that was me who called you out here?

TAXI: Well—I don't know who it was but—

HENRY: Well, it *was* me. Why beat around the bush about it?

TAXI: It was you?

HENRY: Course it was. You don't see anybody else around here, do ya?

TAXI: Well, I'm ready, Mr. Moss.

HENRY: Yeah, yeah, yeah. You're ready. You're ready. Sure. You're always ready. Suppose you got the meter runnin' out there too, huh? Rackin' it up for air time! Click-clocking away!

TAXI: Well, the Company says you gotta—

HENRY: Fuck the Company, all right! Fuck the Company right where it fits. What're you, a Company man? Is that what you are?

TAXI: No, sir, I'm—

HENRY: Are you a Company man or are you your own man? That's the question. What is it? You can't have it both ways.

TAXI: I'm my own—

HENRY: You don't have a clue, buster.

TAXI: I just need some kind of insurance that you actually want the cab—

HENRY: Insurance! Money, you mean? Cash money? That's what you're worried about?

TAXI: No, I—[*Henry starts digging cash out of his pockets. He crosses to table and slams it down.*]

HENRY: Cash money! Mean green! How 'bout that! Look at that! Where would a desperate man come up with so much cash! Surprised ya, huh? Give ya a start?

TAXI: No, sir.

HENRY: That's blood money right there, Mr. Taxi! World War II blood money! Guess how many dead Japs that cost? Take a guess.

TAXI: I, uh—

HENRY: Beyond your imagination, bud. Beyond your imagination.

TAXI: Well, I didn't think you didn't have any money, Mr. Moss. That wasn't what I meant.

HENRY: You got any women, Taxi? [*Pause. Taxi stares at him.*]

TAXI: Women? You mean—

HENRY: I mean, women. The female kind.

TAXI: Well, I've got a girlfriend, if that's what you mean.

HENRY: Girlfriend? Don't gimme that shit. "Girlfriend." I mean *women*. Women women. *Real* women!

TAXI: Well—she's real, all right.

HENRY: I got one. I got a doozy. Make yer tail swim, Taxi. Know what she did to me? You wanna know? Guess. Bet you'll never guess.

TAXI: Mr. Moss, I gotta—

HENRY: She pronounced me dead! That's what she did. [*Pause.*]

TAXI: Dead?

HENRY: That's it. Dead. Ever heard of such a thing? That's what she did to me. Can you imagine? Right in jail too. In front of everyone. We were both incarcerated together and she made that pronouncement. Publicly! Standing right over my semiconscious body. She just bellowed it out to the general jail community at large: "Señor Moss is dead!" Now it's all over town. All over this territory. Everyone thinks I'm dead! [*Pause. Henry grabs bottle again; drinks. Taxi just stands there.*]

TAXI: Well—They must know she was lying by now, don't they?

HENRY: On the contrary! *Nobody* thinks she was lying. Not a single solitary soul.

TAXI: Well—I mean—You're not dead, so—

HENRY: *You* think I'm not dead. That's *you*. But you're not from around here, are you?

TAXI: No, sir, but—

HENRY: You're from Albuquerque.

TAXI: Yes, sir.

HENRY: So what difference does it make what you think? I'm talkin' about the ones right around here. The real ones. They're all that count. All the local ones. I'm a well-known figure around here, in case you didn't know that, buster. They all think I'm dead now on account a her.

TAXI: Well, don't they see you walking around and talking and everything?

HENRY: Walking around and talking? What the hell difference does that make? There's a whole shitload of "walkers" and "talkers"—fabricating and perambulating their butts off! You think they're all in the land of the living? Is that what you think? Huh?

TAXI: I know, but usually—

HENRY: Usually nothin'! There's nothin' usual about this! I'm in a serious jam on account of this woman! She's trying to obliterate me before my natural time! She took out an obituary in the paper: "Henry Jamison Moss; Dead. Deceased. Causes unknown." She did that to me.

TAXI: Well, can't you just explain to everyone that she was mistaken?

HENRY: What's the situation look like to you, bub? Do I look like a dead man or what?

TAXI: No, sir.

HENRY: Not the least bit, huh? Not around the eyes a little? Look around the eyes. That's what gives it away. Look closely here. Come over and give it a good hard look-see. [*Taxi reluctantly approaches Henry and stops in front of him, staring hard at Henry's eyes.*]

HENRY: No, you've got to get in here close! Scrutinize this. Penetrate past the outer covering. [*Taxi moves in closer and bends in toward Henry's face, staring hard at his eyes. Henry opens his eyes wide, using his fingers and thumbs to pry them open.*]

HENRY: Now—Look right deep into the pupil, where it's dark. Where it drops off into nowhere. You see that? Right straight in there like you were riding a train into a black tunnel. What do you see? Tell me what you see. [*Pause. Taxi stares hard into Henry's eyes.*]

TAXI: Nothing. [*Henry drops his hands from his eyes.*]

HENRY: Exactly! Exactly my point. Absolutely nothing!

TAXI: No, I mean, they look okay to me.

HENRY: They look dead!

TAXI: No, sir—

HENRY: Don't jerk my chain, Taxi-man! You're a lyin' dog! Yer from Albuquerque! [*Taxi backs off from Henry.*]

TAXI: Are you ready to go someplace, Mr. Moss, because—I've gotta head on back if you don't need the cab. [*Henry moves in front of him fast and stops him.*]

HENRY: Not so fast, not so fast, not so fast!

TAXI: I can't be just—hanging around here, Mr. Moss. There's other customers waiting. [*Pause. Henry pats Taxi on the shoulder.*]

HENRY: So—Just from your—casual observation, you think there might be a little spark inside there, huh? [*Pointing to his eyes.*] A little ember of hope?

TAXI: You're not dead, all right! As far as I can tell you are not dead! [*Pause.*]

HENRY: Good that's good. That's the first positive note I've heard in months. Tell ya what we're gonna do—Tell ya what, Taxi. Here's what we're gonna do—Ya like to trout fish?

TAXI: Well—sure. Haven't done it in a while, but—

HENRY: Well, that's what we're gonna do, then. Conchalla likes to trout fish too. We're gonna go pick her up and hit the river. You can take it up with her.

TAXI: Conchalla?

HENRY: That's right. Conchalla Lupina. That's the woman. The woman I was referring to. You can take the whole issue up with her out on the Pecos. [*Henry grabs Taxi by the shoulder and starts to weave toward the door.*]

TAXI: What issue?

HENRY: The question of my being! My aliveness! My actuality in this world! Whether or not I'm dead or not! What the hell've we been talkin' about here? Pay attention to the subject!

TAXI: But, I'm not—

HENRY: Just get that cab fired up, bub! Get those pistons rockin'! You'll see. Conchalla's a very influential woman around here. Sharp as jailhouse coffee. You can have it out with her, toe to toe. You can argue my case for me. I've got no one else. Couple a lame-brain sons who couldn't find their peckers in a pickle jar. Take hold of my arm now, boy. Take ahold! [*Taxi grabs Henry's arm.*]

HENRY: That feel like a living arm to you?

TAXI: Yes, sir. It does.

HENRY: Attaboy! You tell her that for me. She might just listen to an outsider from Albuquerque. She might just listen. [*Henry staggers out through door and disappears, leaving Taxi behind. Taxi closes door and turns to face Ray, who remains seated, facing audience. Lights return to previous setup. Ray takes a drink. Pause. He keeps staring out at audience with his back to Taxi.*]

RAY: That's it? That's all you can remember?

TAXI: [*Stays by door.*] That's pretty much it. Yeah.

RAY: No more details?

TAXI: Details? Like what?

RAY: Are you still on your spot? Your same spot?

TAXI: What spot?

RAY: Your spot by the door where I told you to stay.

TAXI: [*Adjusting.*] Oh—Yeah. Yeah, I'm still there. [*Taxi jumps into position. Pause.*]

RAY: Good. That's very good. [*Pause. Ray gets up from chair and crosses to Henry's bed. He sits on bed, facing audience. Pause.*]

TAXI: Look—why don't I just give you the hundred bucks back, okay? [*He digs in his pocket and pulls out money.*] I'll keep the Tiger Rose and we'll call it even-steven. Just for the trip out here. Gas and time involved. We'll write that off. How's that sound?

RAY: [*Laughs.*] "Even-steven"? [*Pause. Ray goes silent. Taxi moves very cautiously toward Ray, holding out the money to him.*]

TAXI: That sound fair to you? I mean—I don't think this is gonna work out, personally. I just got a feeling—I mean, I had a whole different idea about this. Here. [*Offering money to Ray.*] How about it?

RAY: You keep that money, Taxi-man. That's your money. You put it back in your pocket. I don't want it. You put it in your pocket and go back to the door, like I told you, and stay there. All right?

TAXI: Oh no—

RAY: Go back to the door. [*Pause. Taxi slowly puts money back in his pocket, returns to his spot by the door and stands there. He stares at Ray, trembling slightly. Pause. Ray stares out.*]

TAXI: Thing I'm gonna do is go back to Texas. Never shoulda left Texas in the first place. That's the whole problem, right there. I don't fit up here in this country. You get raised up in a friendly place, you think the whole rest of the world's just as friendly. Boy, are you sadly mistaken. [*Ray stands slowly from bed and moves to refrigerator. Taxi stays.*]

RAY: You're not from Texas. You're from Albuquerque.

TAXI: I'm originally from Texas. Tyler, Texas—born and raised. [*Ray opens refrigerator and stares into it.*]

RAY: Texans don't whine. No whiners down in Texas. They kicked 'em all out.

TAXI: What do you know about it? My great-great-grandmother was slaughtered by Comanches. I guess that makes me from Texas, all right.

RAY: [*Looking in fridge.*] Your great-great-grandmother?

TAXI: That's right.

RAY: Your great-great-grandmother was slaughtered by Comanches? Sounds like a story to me.

TAXI: A story?

RAY: A fabrication, passed down from one generation to another. Sounds like that kind of a story. A prideful story.

TAXI: Prideful? There's nothin' prideful about being slaughtered. [*Ray takes out the jar of jalapeños and slams refrigerator door shut. He opens jar, takes out a pepper, pops it in his mouth, then crosses slowly toward Taxi with the jar. Taxi stays.*]

RAY: [*Slowly crossing to Taxi.*] Thing about that kind of a story, Taxi-man, is that the very first fabricator—the original liar who started this little rumor about your slaughtered great-great-grandma—he's dead and gone now, right? Vanished from this earth! All the ones who knew him are dead and gone. All that's left is a cracked tintype, maybe; a gnarly lock of bloody hair; some fingernail clippings in a leather pouch. So there's really no way to verify this little story of yours, is there? This little history. [*Pause. Ray stops very close to Taxi's face, chewing on the pepper.*]

TAXI: You're not calling me a liar, are you?

RAY: Your whole family's a pack of liars. They were born liars. They couldn't help themselves. That's why it's important to try to get at the heart of things, don't you think? Somebody, somewhere along the line has to try to get at the heart of things. [*Pause. They stare at each other, then Ray offers jar of peppers out to Taxi.*]

RAY: Jalapeño?

TAXI: No. Thank you.

RAY: Come on, now! You're from Texas! You can take a little heat. [*Ray slowly takes out a jalapeño and pushes it into Taxi's mouth. Taxi chews. Ray moves away from him to table and sits. Taxi starts quietly choking on pepper, eyes watering, breaking out in a sweat. He wants to grab the bottle off the table to cool the fire but is afraid to move from his spot.*]

RAY: [*Seated at table.*] No way to verify this story at all. It's like my brother. Just like my brother. He's a fabricator too. He makes something up out of thin air, thinking I'll fall for it.

Just swallow it whole. No questions: "Dad's dead." That's how he put it. "Dad's dead." Simple as that. End of issue.

TAXI: [*Choking, gasping for air.*] Could—Could I—Could I get my bottle, please? Do you think—[*Pause. Ray stares at him as he chokes, then slides bottle in Taxi's direction. Taxi hesitates to leave his spot, but Ray gestures for him to go ahead and take bottle. Taxi lunges for bottle, takes a huge swig, clears his throat and stares at Ray, his eyes popping from the heat.*]

TAXI: Thanks.

RAY: You go back over to your spot now, Taxi.

TAXI: Oh, no—Couldn't we—just be friendly?

RAY: You just go on back over there. You remember where it is, don't you?

TAXI: What? My—my—spot?

RAY: Yeah. [*Pause. Taxi moves back to his spot by door; turns to Ray.*]

TAXI: Was this it?

RAY: Close enough.

TAXI: Look—I've got this terrible feeling all of a sudden. I—I mean I—I don't know anything. I didn't think there was anything wrong here to begin with. I mean when I first came over, you know. I wouldn't have volunteered for this if I thought there was anything wrong here. I just—I don't—I gotta go now. I really gotta go—[*Taxi moves to door as though to exit. Ray suddenly flies at him from the chair and pins him up*

*against the door. Ray grabs him by the chest. Taxi offers no
resistance; just whimpers.*]

RAY: [*Close to Taxi's face.*] I didn't give you a hundred bucks
and a bottle of Tiger Rose so you could skip out on me!
What'd you think this was, a free ride? Huh! Is that what
you thought?

TAXI: I don't want the hundred bucks! I told you that!

RAY: You took it! It's too late now. You owe me. You're in debt
to me. You're deeply in debt!

TAXI: Oh, my God! Oh, my God in heaven. [*Pause. Ray lets go of
him and backs off slowly but stands near him. Taxi slumps back
against door; his head bows like he's on the verge of breaking
down. He trembles all over.*]

TAXI: I need to get back and see my girlfriend!

RAY: You don't have a girlfriend.

TAXI: I do! I do too! I do so have a girlfriend! I'm from Texas
and I've got a girlfriend! How come you're trying to take
everything away from me? I don't wanna be here! I don't
wanna be here at all! I want—I wanna leave now! I wanna go!

RAY: Yeah, but you owe me something now, Taxi. You owe me
a little story.

TAXI: What story?

RAY: The story of when you all returned; the returning story.
When you came back here. To this place, right here. With
my dad and this woman and a string of fish. [*Short pause,*

then Conchalla bursts through the door, knocking Taxi toward the bed. Henry stumbles through, close behind her, holding up a very small fish by the tail. Ray moves extreme downstage right and stands, facing audience throughout flashback. The other characters ignore him. Taxi falls in with Henry and Conchalla as an active member of the flashback. Conchalla is extremely drunk and singing loudly in some strange dialect that sounds like a mixture of Spanish and Indian. She carries a bottle of tequila and heads straight for the tub, pushing Taxi out of her way. She turns the hot water on full blast and starts taking her skirt and blouse off as she continues to sing. Henry stumbles to the table, as drunk as Conchalla, and flops the fish down on it. He picks the fish up and starts flopping it back and forth on the table as he sings in competition with Conchalla.]

HENRY: [*Singing loudly.*]
  Gonna tie my pecker to a tree, to a tree
  Gonna tie my pecker to a tree
  Gonna tie my pecker to a tree, to a tree
  Gonna tie my pecker to a tree.
[*Pause as Henry looks around the room, ignoring Ray. Conchalla goes into humming her song and continues getting ready for her bath. She drinks from bottle and takes some kind of oil out of her belt and starts oiling her skin as the water steams in the tub. Taxi looks on.*]

HENRY: Look at this fish! Now, that's a fish! [*Henry holds the tiny fish up as though it were a trophy. Conchalla laughs.*]

CONCHALLA: That is no fish! That is fish wishing to become a fish. A wish fish!

HENRY: [*Turning toward Conchalla, weaving.*] I knew—I just knew—Now, how did I know that you were gonna rain on my rainbow like that? How'd I know that?

CONCHALLA: That is a minnow! That is a bait fish, maybe.

HENRY: [*Holding up fish.*] That's a legitimate fish right there! Wouldn't you say that was a legitimate fish, Taxi? That's a fish!

TAXI: Well, yeah—it's a fish but—you probably shoulda let him grow some.

HENRY: Let him grow? What the hell good's that? Let him grow! Ya mean throw him back is what ya mean. That's what ya mean, isn't it? Throw him back. [*To Conchalla.*] He wants me to throw back my catch of the day.

CONCHALLA: That is no fish. Dead men cannot catch fish. Dead men have no need to fish. They are never hungry. [*Conchalla starts laughing and climbs into steaming tub.*]

HENRY: Don't start that up again with me! There she goes! There she goes again!

TAXI: Mr. Moss, I was wondering if maybe you could pay me for the trip now and I could—[*Henry ignores Taxi. He takes fish over to Conchalla in the tub and starts waving it in her face as Conchalla bathes.*]

HENRY: She just refuses to recognize the simple truth of the thing. This is a genuine fish! A trophy fish! Look at the size of this fish!

CONCHALLA: I remember he bragged the same way about his penis.

HENRY: I never bragged about my penis! That's an outright lie! I never did that. [*To Taxi.*] She's lying again. Look at this fish!

CONCHALLA: That is a silly fish. That is a silly, silly fish. [*Conchalla suddenly snatches the fish out of Henry's grasp and flips it into the steaming water of the tub.*]

HENRY: [*To Taxi.*] Did you see that? Did you see what she did?

TAXI: Mr. Moss, I gotta get back to my girlfriend. I mean she's—

HENRY: She just threw my fish into the steaming water! My one and only fish!

CONCHALLA: There was no fish. You must have been dreaming!

HENRY: There was a fish! Everyone knows there was a fish! [*Henry makes a move toward Conchalla to retrieve his fish.*]

CONCHALLA: [*Fierce; her voice drops an octave.*] Don't you come near this fish!! [*Henry freezes.*] I have it between my thighs now.

HENRY: Oh, she's disgusting.

CONCHALLA: Do you want it to come back to life?

HENRY: No! I don't want it to come back to life! I caught it! It's dead. I want it to stay dead.

CONCHALLA: I can bring it back to life for you. It is easy.

HENRY: I don't want it brought back to life! I'm gonna fry it up.

CONCHALLA: I just squeeze him a little between my legs. Like this—

HENRY: No!

TAXI: Mr. Moss, do you think we might be able to settle up here now? I need to get my money! I don't know how many times I gotta tell you.

HENRY: You'll get yer damn money! Not that you deserve it. What've you been doin' fer yer money? Huh? Sittin' around choking yer chicken! That's about it. Watching her continue to insult and berate me up one side of the river and down the other. Not once did you ever make so much as a gesture on my behalf! Not once!

TAXI: I'm a driver! I'm a taxicab driver! That's what I do. I drive people around from one place to another. That's all I do. I don't know about anything else. I don't know what you expect from me.

HENRY: I expect you to make a stand! That's what I expect. I've expected it all along! You told me you saw something in here. [*Points to his eyes.*] Something glimmering.

TAXI: I never said I saw something glimmering!

HENRY: That's what you said.

TAXI: I never said that!

HENRY: What'd you say, then?

TAXI: I said I saw nothing! Zero! Goose eggs. Absolutely nothing. It looked like a plain old everyday eyeball to me.

HENRY: I'm surrounded by liars! She says there's no fish, then there is a fish.

CONCHALLA: [*Laughs, looks down between her legs.*] It's starting to swim now.

HENRY: It can't be! It's dead. [*Henry moves toward Conchalla, but she stops him with a gesture.*]

CONCHALLA: [*Looking down at fish.*] Come take a look at your fish. It's peaceful now. It's happy. It has found its place in this world. Look at it swimming. Swimming, swimming. [*Pause.*]

TAXI: Mr. Moss, look—If you're not going to give me the money—I mean—just tell me what you want me to do. Just tell me and I'll do it. Okay? Then you can pay me and I'll get outta here. How's that sound? What exactly is it that you wanna convince her of?

HENRY: You ever been with a woman who thought you were dead?

TAXI: Well, no—I guess not. No.

HENRY: Then you don't know what it's like, do ya?

TAXI: No, sir but—I mean, there must've been a time when she thought you were alive. Right?

HENRY: I can't remember.

TAXI: Well—think back. Maybe if you could remember, then I could try to remind her.

HENRY: Remind her of what?

TAXI: Whatever it was. Was it your walk or something?

75

HENRY: My walk?

TAXI: Your talk?

HENRY: My talk?

TAXI: Well, I don't know—Was it your smile, maybe?

HENRY: [*Pushes Taxi away.*] Don't be an idiot!

TAXI: I'm just trying to help, is all!

HENRY: You're not trying to help! All you care about is your money! Your lousy money!

TAXI: I don't know exactly what it is you want me to do.

HENRY: Here's what I want you to do. Walk right over to her. Go ahead. Walk right over there to her, like a man, and explain the situation.

TAXI: What situation?

HENRY: What is the matter with you?

TAXI: You mean, explain to her that you're not dead?

HENRY: That's the ticket!

TAXI: How come you don't know that you're not dead? I don't get that.

HENRY: I know that I'm not dead! She's the one who doesn't know that I'm not dead! Now get on over there! Just take the plunge. [*Pause. Taxi very tentatively approaches Conchalla as she hums softly in the tub, oblivious to the others. Taxi stops. Taxi inches closer to Conchalla, who has her eyes closed, head resting back against the tub, very peaceful.*]

TAXI: Uh—Miss Lupina? [*No response from Conchalla. She just smiles, keeps her eyes closed and hums softly.*]

TAXI: Uh—ma'am—You don't really know me but—I'm—I'm the type a guy who calls a spade a spade. You know? I mean, I'm a pretty levelheaded, honest type a guy and—

HENRY: She doesn't give a shit what type a guy you are! You're supposed to be telling her about me! What about me?

TAXI: I was getting to that. I was just—Uh—Miss Lupina—There are certain signs of life that I think we can all agree on, aren't there? I mean, when you see someone breathing and—yelling and—

HENRY: Breathing and yelling? Breathing and yelling!

TAXI: [*To Henry.*] Yeah! Yeah, I mean, that's what you're doing! You're breathing and yelling so—

HENRY: That's not what I wanna be known for—Breathing and yelling! What the hell is that! I've got lots of qualities besides breathing and yelling! Tell her about those!

TAXI: I haven't seen those. [*Suddenly Conchalla lets out a gasp and raises her arm up out of the water with the fish dangling from her fingers. The fish is alive and twitching. She raises the fish directly over her head. Her eyes open, her mouth opens wide. Short pause, then she lets the fish drop directly into her mouth.*

Her jaws close as she grinds the fish between her teeth. Her arm drops with a mighty splash. Her eyes close again. She smiles as she goes on chewing the fish. Taxi runs toward the door, in terror. Henry storms toward Conchalla, but she remains undisturbed.]

HENRY: [*To Conchalla.*] That was my fish she just ate!

TAXI: [*By door.*] All right! That's it! That's it—I'm leaving! This is not good for me! My girlfriend would not like me to be here with you people! She warned me about people like you. [*Suddenly the door swings open, almost knocking Taxi over. Esteban stands there in doorway with another bowl of steaming soup. Pause.*]

HENRY: [*To Esteban.*] What the hell're you doing here?

ESTEBAN: [*Smiling.*] Mr. Henry, I brought you some soup.

HENRY: I don't want any goddamn soup now! What're you doin', barging in here with soup? Can't you see we're busy! We're busy here!

ESTEBAN: [*Still in doorway.*] I saw the taxi and—I came over. I was worried for you.

CONCHALLA: [*From tub.*] Don't worry for the dead! Worry for the living!

ESTEBAN: Oh—She is here? Conchalla is here? [*Esteban gets very excited and steps into room, looking toward Conchalla.*]

HENRY: Yeah, she's here! She ate my fish! [*Conchalla cackles and splashes in the tub. Esteban heads toward her, slowly, carrying the soup in front of him.*]

ESTEBAN: I would have brought two bowls of soup. I did not know she was here.

CONCHALLA: Dead men can't eat soup!

HENRY: [*To Conchalla.*] Shut up with that!

TAXI: Mr. Moss, I'm asking you for the last time for my money. Ninety-six dollars and forty-two cents. That's what you owe me. [*Henry starts pulling out crumpled wet bills from his pockets and handing them over to Taxi as he speaks. Esteban keeps heading toward Conchalla, completely enraptured with her presence. Conchalla trickles water down her arms and sings to herself softly.*]

HENRY: All right, all right, all right! Stop whimpering about yer damn money.

ESTEBAN: If only I had known you were here. I would have made my *carne asada.*

HENRY: [*As he hands over money to Taxi.*] What did I ever do to deserve this? I've led an honorable life for the most part. I've served my country. I've dropped bombs on total strangers! I've worked my ass off for idiots. Paid my taxes. There's never once been any question of my—existence! Never once. It's humiliating! A man my age—to be forced into this kind of position. I'm too old to be having to prove I'm alive!

CONCHALLA: [*Laughing, singsong.*] No one will come to his rescue! No one will come to his rescue.

ESTEBAN: The voice of an angel. [*Henry now seems to be talking to himself more than anyone else; staggering around, still doling out money to Taxi, who keeps counting it and asking for more. Esteban becomes more and more hypnotized by Conchalla.*]

HENRY: It's true—Maybe it's true—Maybe I am on the dark side of the moon now. It's possible. Maybe I am just—just completely—gone. [*Henry appeals to Esteban, but Esteban is locked onto Conchalla with his eyes. Taxi only wants the money. Suddenly Earl appears in the open doorway, extremely drunk. Henry freezes and stares at him. Ray immediately reacts to Earl's presence but still remains outside the action. He turns to face Earl, but Earl ignores him. Short pause as Earl just stands there, weaving slightly in doorway. Conchalla becomes alarmed at Earl's presence. She stands in the tub and yells at Esteban, who immediately reacts.*]

CONCHALLA: Get me my blanket! I need my blanket now! No one can even take a bath in peace. [*Esteban sets down the soup, rushes to bed and pulls the blanket off it, then takes it to Conchalla, who snatches it away from him and wraps herself up in it. She stays standing in tub. Henry staggers toward Earl.*]

HENRY: [*To Earl.*] What the hell're you doing, standing in my doorway? Who're you supposed to be?

EARL: I'm supposed to be your oldest son. That's who I'm supposed to be.

HENRY: [*Turning to Esteban.*] What is this? What's going on here?

ESTEBAN: I called him, Mr. Henry. I did not know what to do.

HENRY: [*Approaching Esteban.*] You called him?

ESTEBAN: I was worried something bad might have happened to you.

HENRY: Something bad? Something bad *has* just happened to me. Something bad *is* happening to me. Treachery from every angle! Sons! Neighbors! Women! Family! There's no end to it! How's a man supposed to breathe? [*Taxi exits and closes door behind him. When the door closes, suddenly everyone freezes except Ray, who slowly crosses over to Earl and stops right in front of him, very close. He stares at Earl, then slowly reaches out and opens Earl's eyes very wide with his fingers and thumbs. This gesture should be reminiscent of Henry opening his eyes wide for Taxi to examine. Pause.*]

RAY: I see you, Earl. I see you now. [*Lights fade fast to black.*]

Act Three

Scene: *Next morning. Same set. The photo album and tool chest are gone. Esteban is cooking menudo in a black pot on the stove. He has his spices, herbs and wears an orange apron. He is very meticulous and attentive to his cooking. Earl has a raging hangover. He lies on his back on Henry's bed, holding his head with both hands and writhing with pain. He moans and tries, with no effect, to kick his boots off. Esteban hums a sweet tune as he cooks. (Note: The cooking should be actual so that the smells of the menudo fill the room.)*

EARL: [*Calling out to Esteban.*] The shoes! The shoes! Help me off with the damn shoes! [*Esteban reluctantly leaves his pot and goes to help Earl. He starts trying to pull Earl's boots off as Earl moans.*]

ESTEBAN: Oh, Mr. Earl, why you no come home when I tell you? Is no good to drink so much like that. You drink enough for ten men. We should have come home right after we make the phone call. Now we have miss everyone. Your father is gone. Your brother is gone.

EARL: [*Struggling to kick his boots off.*] They've always been gone! They were never here to begin with!

ESTEBAN: I feel bad we no here when your father they take him away. We should have been here for that, Mr. Earl. To see your father off.

EARL: [*Kicking out at Esteban.*] Get away from me! Just get the hell away! It's like being with a woman, being around you!

82

ESTEBAN: You cry for help—You chase me away. You chase me away—You cry for help. It's the same as your father.

EARL: [*Sitting up with a struggle.*] I am *nothing* like the old man! Get that into your fry-brain little mind! We're as different as chalk and cheese! I am *nothing* like the old man! [*Esteban backs off and returns to his cooking. Pause as Earl finishes kicking off one boot. He sits up on edge of bed, tries to steady his dizziness, clutches his head in agony.*]

EARL: Oh, my God! Feels like an ax in the back of my head. How'd you allow me to get into this kinda condition? Huh? You watch after Henry like a damn nanny goat, then you just turn my ass loose in every strange bar in creation. Where in the hell are your sense of values, man?

ESTEBAN: You wanted to go to those bars, Mr. Earl. You wanted to visit all of Henry's old bars. That's what you told me.

EARL: Now, why would I tell you something like that? Why would I give a shit about Henry's old bars?

ESTEBAN: You are asking me this?

EARL: I'm asking you. Yeah.

ESTEBAN: Menudo is almost ready.

EARL: I don't want any goddamn menudo! I'm asking you a question! Why would I wanna go around to Henry's old bars?

ESTEBAN: I have no idea, Mr. Earl. Maybe you thought you would—discover something.

EARL: Discover? Discover what?

ESTEBAN: Something about Henry.

EARL: [*Gives up pursuit.*] Ah, shit.

ESTEBAN: Menudo will cure you.

EARL: I told you, I don't want any a that goddamn stuff! What is that junk anyway? Boiled cow bellies? Where do you people come up with this shit? Who first thought of that? Boiled cow intestines! Jesus. It's primitive.

ESTEBAN: It will take away the pain.

EARL: I'm not eating any boiled cow guts! The brain of a man does not respond to the guts of a cow! Don't you know anything? [*Pause. Esteban keeps stirring the menudo. Earl nurses his head.*]

ESTEBAN: You are right about one thing.

EARL: What's that?

ESTEBAN: You are nothing like your father. You are worse than your father. At least with Henry you could have a conversation.

EARL: Oh yeah, he was a real conversationalist, wasn't he? Real gift for gab, old Henry. Just talk your head off on any damn subject. [*Pause.*] What was in it for you, anyway?

ESTEBAN: *Mande?*

EARL: What was in it for you? You and Henry. I mean all that—sacrifice. Taking all that shit off a him all that time. What'd you ever have coming back?

ESTEBAN: [*Keeps stirring pot.*] I no understand, Mr. Earl.

EARL: What satisfaction could you possibly get outta serving a man who was so damn ungrateful!

ESTEBAN: It is like—feeding livestock—you know?

EARL: Feeding livestock?

ESTEBAN: Birds.

EARL: Birds?

ESTEBAN: They do nothing. They—live, that is all. They are just there. But they need you. They look to you. They wait for you by the fence. They know you bring them something. Every day they are there at the same time—waiting. They know the hour you will appear. Mr. Henry, he use to wait for me like that. I would see him standing by that window, looking toward my trailer. I would never tell him I see him waiting like that. He would be embarrassed; angry. But he look for me. I was the only one. He have no one else. Then—sometimes late at night, I come over and we sit. We just sit here at that table, facing the moon. We listen to the radio. We no speak. Sometimes we no speak for hours. Just listen. Music from deep in Mexico.

EARL: But every now and then you'd have a conversation—right? You were saying you used to have conversations—

ESTEBAN: Sometimes. Sometimes Henry he ask me about my pueblo—Where I come from. My people, my family. He never talk about himself. He say he have no past. Mostly we just listen. Dogs. Coyotes. *La música*. It was peaceful.

EARL: Peaceful? Henry?

ESTEBAN: The two of us.

EARL: Peaceful. That'd be something, wouldn't it?

ESTEBAN: What?

EARL: Peace. [*Pause.*]

ESTEBAN: Ay. Menudo. [*Returns to stove. Esteban keeps stirring pot. Earl gazes around room, then suddenly notices the missing toolbox and photo album. He stands fast and moves shakily toward table.*]

EARL: That sonofabitch took everything! Look! He took the tools and the album. And the bottle! He took the damn bottle too! Those didn't belong to him! Nobody said he could have that stuff! Who in the hell does he think he is? He's absconded with everything! Look at this!

ESTEBAN: Maybe he was only cleaning up.

EARL: Cleaning up? He's ripped me off! He doesn't deserve any of that stuff! That was mine! That belonged to me! I inherited it fair and square! I was the one who stuck it out here with Henry. Not him!

ESTEBAN: I am very sorry we miss him. I wanted to say good-bye.

EARL: Who?

ESTEBAN: Mr. Henry.

EARL: He was dead! You don't say good-bye to a dead man! It's too late. I'm talking about my brother now. My living, breathing conniving brother!

ESTEBAN: In my village we always say good-bye to the dead.

EARL: This is not your village. We're across the river here.

ESTEBAN: They will come back to haunt you if you do not say good-bye.

EARL: Will you knock it off with that! Dead is dead, all right? Finished. *Terminado.*

ESTEBAN: Maybe.

EARL: Maybe nothing.

ESTEBAN: Maybe Henry was waiting to say good-bye and we weren't here.

EARL: Jesus H. Christ! Just—Just—stir your damn pot, will you! Just—[*Earl sits down heavily in upstage chair and holds his throbbing head between his hands. Long pause as Esteban continues to stir his pot.*]

ESTEBAN: [*Stirring.*] We had a cousin, Manolito, once, who died from a green snake. No one said good-bye to him. There was superstition about the snake and no one said good-bye. The next day a hawk appeared above the door of his uncle's house. Every day the hawk would shit on his uncle's head just as he stepped outside. Every single day. That went on for over a month. This is the kind of thing that can happen when you don't say good-bye to the dead. You get shit on by a hawk. [*Short pause. Earl lowers his hands and looks at Esteban. Suddenly Ray enters with a bag of groceries and closes door behind him. He stops and stares at Earl. Earl stays seated. Esteban turns and stares at Ray.*]

RAY: How's it going? [*Ray crosses to refrigerator, opens it and starts unloading groceries into it. Pause.*]

EARL: "How's it going?" That's all you've got to say? "How's it going?"

RAY: [*Unloading groceries.*] Well, I was thinking about "How ya doing?" or "What's goin' on?" or "Where you been so long?" or—

EARL: What're you doing back here?

RAY: Stockin' up the larder. Puttin' in a few supplies. I made kind of a big decision last night. It just came on me.

EARL: Yeah, what decision's that?

RAY: I'm gonna stay awhile. [*Pause. Earl stares at Ray, who keeps unloading groceries and putting them in fridge. Esteban keeps stirring.*]

EARL: You're gonna stay?

RAY: Yep.

EARL: You mean here? You're gonna stay here in this house? Henry's house?

88

RAY: Yep. I like it here.

EARL: Oh, so now you like it here. It's warm and cozy.

RAY: I dunno. I feel—some kind of connection here.

EARL: Connection?

RAY: Yep.

EARL: I suppose you felt some kind of "connection" to the tools and the photo album too, huh? And the bottle. *My* bottle.

RAY: Oh—Yeah, well—I gave those away.

EARL: [*Moving toward Ray.*] What?

RAY: I gave 'em away to that taxicab driver.

EARL: What taxicab driver!

RAY: You know, the guy who uh—took Dad fishing. [*Pause.*]

EARL: What're you talking about?

RAY: The guy—the driver who came and picked Dad up. You know. [*Pause.*]

EARL: You—found him?

RAY: Yep.

EARL: What do you mean? How'd you find him?

RAY: Tracked him down. Like I said. Through the company. Made some phone calls down there at the Sonic. I looked all over the place for you guys but I guess you were, uh–"celebrating" or something, huh?

EARL: You found the taxicab driver who took Henry fishing?

RAY: That's what I said, yeah. Amazing huh?

EARL: You actually went all the way out of your way to find the taxicab driver who took Henry fishing? [*Ray finishes with groceries, closes refrigerator, takes a Coke with him, crosses to Earl, stops in front of Earl and raps on Earl's forehead like he was knocking on a door.*]

RAY: What is it, Earl–liquor or genetics that makes you so thick? [*Ray crosses to table, sits and opens Coke, takes a drink.*]

EARL: So–So what'd he do? You talk to him?

RAY: Yeah. Sure I talked to him. What is that stink?

ESTEBAN: Menudo.

RAY: Really stinks.

EARL: [*Moving toward Ray.*] So, what'd he say–this taxicab driver? He tell you anything different than what I told you?

RAY: Now why would he do that?

EARL: I don't know why he'd do that! Just to–confuse the issue probably. People are always making up stuff.

RAY: What issue?

EARL: You know—the *issue*—the whole situation. The perdicament here!

RAY: I didn't know there was a perdicament here, Earl.

EARL: There isn't a perdicament here but he could've made it seem like there was a perdicament here! He could've twisted things around!

RAY: He just told me what happened, that's all. Simple story.

EARL: [*Pause.*] So—Everything matched up, right? I mean— everything he told you was the same thing I told you, right?

RAY: Pretty much. [*Pause.*]

EARL: What the hell are you doing giving away our father's belongings to a complete stranger? That's what I wanna know. What kind of a stunt is that?

RAY: I didn't think they meant anything to you.

EARL: There were photographs in there going back to the turn of the century!

RAY: Yeah. That's a long time ago.

EARL: You're goddamn right that's a long time ago! Those photographs are irreplaceable. Now some total stranger's got ahold of them. An outsider!

RAY: Well, he can always make up some kind of a story about them.

EARL: What's that supposed to mean?

RAY: He can tell people they're pictures of *his* family. *His* ancestors. He can make up a whole tall tale.

EARL: Why would he wanna do that?

RAY: Maybe he's got no family. Maybe he needs to make one up.

EARL: If he's got no family he can't make one up! That's not something you make up outta thin air! You can't make that stuff up. It's too complicated!

RAY: People will believe anything, Earl. You know that. Look at all the stuff you've told me.

EARL: What stuff?

RAY: Over the years. All the bullshit you've told me. I believed every word.

EARL: You know what? You're beginning to make me a little bit sick to my stomach. Ever since you arrived here—You come in here with this—this—"atmosphere" around you. This suspicion. Right off the bat. Everybody's under suspicion. You don't have one clue about what's gone on here—about what me and Esteban have been through. You just waltz in here and start judging—Passing judgment!

RAY: I've got a clue, Earl. I've got a big clue. [*Pause. The brothers stare at each other. Esteban very quietly stirs his pot, trying to become invisible. Pause. Earl shakes his head in disgust.*]

ESTEBAN: Menudo is almost ready!

EARL: [*Turning on Esteban.*] I don't want any menudo! I told you that! I'm not interested in menudo! If you mention menudo one more time I'm gonna rip your guts out and throw them in that pot! [*Earl clutches his head in pain. He returns to Henry's bed and crashes.*]

EARL: [*Writhing on bed.*] Oh, my God. Oh, my God, my God, my God!!!

RAY: [*At table, sipping Coke.*] Too much party, Earl? You're a little old to be hitting the sauce like that. What were you uh— "celebrating" exactly? The removal of the corpse?

EARL: [*On bed.*] You get outta here now! Go someplace else! There's lots of motels in this town. You just get outta here!

RAY: Or were you uh—thinking maybe you got away with something? [*Pause. Earl struggles to sit up on the bed. He finally makes it and sits there, facing Ray.*]

EARL: What'd this joker tell you? This taxicab driver? He told you something, didn't he?

RAY: Now, what would he tell me, Earl?

EARL: [*Standing, shaky.*] He put some idea in your head!

RAY: I got my own ideas, Earl. I don't need any new ones.

EARL: He was an idiot, that guy! A total idiot!

RAY: Oh, so you met him then? You were here the same time he was, huh?

EARL: I didn't—I didn't meet him! Henry told me about him.

RAY: Henry?

EARL: I mean—Esteban! Esteban told me he was an idiot! [*To Esteban.*] Didn't you? [*No answer from Esteban.*] Didn't you tell me that! You told me the guy was a total jerk.

RAY: Well, which was it—a jerk or an idiot?

EARL: [*To Ray.*] You're trying to turn this thing into something that it wasn't!

RAY: What was it, Earl? What exactly *was* it? [*Earl charges Ray but Ray dodges him quickly and is out of the chair in a flash.*]

EARL: I want you outta here! I want you the hell outta here now! [*Earl crashes into the table and crumples on top of it, exhausted. Ray slowly circles him. Pause. Esteban turns the fire off under his pot. Ray keeps circling Earl, who remains sprawled out on top of the table.*]

ESTEBAN: I will come back later.

RAY: [*Keeps circling.*] No, you just keep cooking, Esteban. No reason to stop cooking.

ESTEBAN: I think I should go back to my trailer, Mr. Ray.

EARL: [*Collapsed on table.*] My legs. I can't feel my legs!

RAY: Get off the table, Earl. What do you think this is, a flop-house or something? A drunk tank!

EARL: Something's happened to my legs!

RAY: Get off the table! [*Ray kicks Earl's feet out from under him. Earl crashes to the floor. Esteban moves toward door. Pause.*]

ESTEBAN: I have no reason to be here, Mr. Ray.

RAY: None of us do, Esteban. That's the truth of it, isn't it? We're all just hanging around now. The old man's dead. [*Esteban crosses back to stove, turns it on and continues stirring pot. Earl stays on floor.*]

EARL: [*On floor.*] Something's really gone wrong with my legs, Ray. I'm not kidding you. I don't know what it is.

RAY: Get up off the floor, Earl. You're a full-grown man.

EARL: [*Stays on floor.*] I—I think we should call somebody.

RAY: Get up off the floor!! [*Ray kicks Earl hard in the ribs. Earl struggles to the downstage chair and drags himself up into it. Esteban keeps stirring.*] You know what I think? I think it's time we straightened up in here, don't you? Get a little order. I mean if I'm gonna be living here I'd like to have a little order. Scrub the floors maybe. The windows. Brighten the place up a bit. What do you think? How 'bout it, Esteban? You got a bucket around? A mop? [*Pause. Esteban and Earl stare at him like he's lost his mind.*]

RAY: No mop?

ESTEBAN: No mop, Mr. Ray.

RAY: No mop. How 'bout some rags, then? Must be some old rags around. Well, this will work. [*Ray rips the apron off Esteban and balls it up. He crosses to Earl, crushing the apron between his hands.*] Now, here's what we're gonna do, Earl. This is my house now. So I want it clean. It's only natural. I want it spotless. I want it so you can eat right off the floor.

So you can see the sun bounce off every little nook and cranny. Now, I want you to take this apron and get it wet. [*Ray grabs Earl by the hair, shoves the apron into Earl's face and drags Earl over to the tub. He turns the hot water on and forces Earl to soak the apron in it.*]

ESTEBAN: [*At stove, crossing himself frantically.*] Jesús, María, José! Jesús, María, José! Jesús, María, José!

RAY: [*At tub, forcing Earl.*] Get it wet now, Earl. Get it nice and wet and wring it out. Scrub every inch of this floor till it shines like new money! That's what I want you to do, Earl. I want you to do that for me, right now. [*Pause. Earl follows Ray's orders. Ray smiles at Esteban and crosses to him. Ray smells the pot of menudo and pats Esteban on the back.*] Stuff really stinks bad, Esteban. Is it supposed to smell like that? Smells like something dead. [*Earl begins slowly scrubbing floor with wet apron, on his hands and knees. Ray moves to tub and shuts the water off.*] This whole house stinks. Why is that? Is that from all your cooking, Esteban—over the years? Years and years of soups and chili and beans and shit? All that cooking. For what? What'd you think you were gonna do? Save Henry's puny life? Is that what you thought?

EARL: I'm really serious about my legs, Ray. They've gone numb. [*Ray suddenly kicks the bed. Earl stops scrubbing but stays on his hands and knees. Esteban is backed up to the stove.*]

RAY: Just keep scrubbing, Earl. We may have to disinfect this whole house. We may have to tear the walls down and rebuild the whole sonbitch. Just to get the stink outta here. What is that stink? Can't you smell that? What smells like that? Maybe it's you, Earl. Is it you that smells like that? [*Earl starts scrub-*

96

bing the floor again. Ray goes to him, bends down and smells Earl all over as Earl continues scrubbing.]

RAY: Esteban—Come over here and smell Earl. See what you think. Come on over here. [*Esteban reluctantly crosses to Earl and Ray.*]

RAY: [*To Esteban.*] Now, just bend down here and smell him. I can't tell anymore. I've lost track. What's he smell like to you? [*Esteban bends over and smells Earl, who continues scrubbing floor. Esteban straightens up and stares at Ray.*]

RAY: Well?

ESTEBAN: Just—like a man, Mr. Ray.

RAY: A man! Is that what a man smells like? [*Ray bends over and takes a long whiff of Earl, who keeps right on scrubbing through all this. Ray straightens up.*] Nah, I dunno—Smells rotten to me. [*Earl stops scrubbing.*]

EARL: Look—I'm not feeling so good. That tequila messed me up. I'm not used to that stuff. [*Ray kicks Earl in the ass.*]

RAY: Keep scrubbing, Earl! Just keep yer nose to the grindstone. There's a lotta territory to cover here. Lots of square footage. [*Earl starts scrubbing floor again. Esteban returns to his place by the stove. Ray moves around the room.*] You remember how Mom used to work at it, don't ya?

EARL: [*Scrubbing.*] Mom?

RAY: Yeah. You remember how she used to scrub, day in and day out. Scrub, scrub, scrub.

EARL: I don't remember.

RAY: You remember. You remember how she used to get everything spit-shined and polished—everything gleaming. The floors. The curtains. The tablecloth starched. All the glasses shining. [*Throughout this sequence the tempo of Earl's scrubbing increases with the force of Ray's pursuit. Ray moves freely around the space.*]

EARL: No—

RAY: You remember. Potatoes steaming on the plates. Carrots. Everything waiting. Everything perfect and just waiting like some kind of picture. You remember all that.

EARL: No—

RAY: And then—I used to think—I used to think she was doing all that for us, you know. You and me. I used to think she was going through all this work—all this preparation for us. And then, one day, it just—hit me. I don't know why. I just suddenly saw that it wasn't for us at all. It was for *him*. It was for Henry. Everything. All those hours and hours, slaving away—Slaving away. It was for him.

EARL: I don't remember that.

RAY: And then—And then, here he'd come! Bustin' in the door. You remember. [*Ray rushes to the door, opens and slams it, then turns himself into drunken Henry, staggering into the room. Earl keeps scrubbing.*]

RAY: [*Impersonating Henry.*] "What the hell is everyone waitin' on me for? What're you waitin' on? The food's hot! Sit down and eat the food. Jesus H. Christ! You'd think this was some kinda goddamn formal dinner here or something. You're hungry aren't ya? Sit down and eat!" [*Drops impersonation.*] And then everybody'd scramble to the table while he'd stomp the shit off his boots and throw his coat on the floor. You remember that? You remember how we'd all just sit there staring down into our napkins while he went on ranting and raving about the lack of rain or the price of citrus or the cost of feeding useless sons! Do you remember that, Earl! Do you remember that at all!!

EARL: [*Still scrubbing.*] No, I don't remember! I don't remember any of that. You must've been alone. I must've been out someplace.

RAY: You were there, Earl. You were there the whole time. I remember your breath. The sound of your breath. Chopping away. I remember thinking, "He must be just as scared as me to be breathing like that. Just as full of terror!" But then I thought, "No, that's not possible. He's bigger than me. He's my big brother. How could he be scared?" And when she started screaming I thought Earl's gonna stand up for her. Earl's gonna take the weight. Earl's gonna stop him somehow!

EARL: I wasn't there for that! I was never there!

RAY: Because I knew, see—I knew I didn't have a chance against him. I barely came up to his waist. All I could do is watch! And there she was—On the floor! Just like you, Earl. Just like you are now. Backed up under the sink! Crushed. He was kicking her, Earl! He was kicking her just like this! [*Ray starts savagely kicking Earl all over the stage. Earl scrambles on his hands and knees but Ray is relentless. Esteban cowers and stays clear.*] And every time he kicked her his rage grew a little bit and his face changed! His eyes bulged out and the blood rushed into his neck! And her blood was flying all over the kitchen, Earl!

EARL: [*Scrambling away on hands and knees.*] That wasn't me that was doing that! That wasn't me! That was him! [*Ray suddenly stops kicking Earl. They are both panting for breath.*]

RAY: And still I kept thinking—I kept thinking—sooner or later Earl's gonna step in. Earl's gonna stop him. Earl's not going to let this happen. And just then—I looked out the kitchen window and I saw your car—your little white Chevy. Kicking up dust the whole length of the hay field. And that's the last time I saw you, Earl. That's the last time I saw you for a long, long while.

EARL: [*Still on floor.*] I never ran! I never ran! [*Short pause, then Henry suddenly blasts through the door with Conchalla close behind, still wrapped up in the blanket. Ray moves immediately extreme downstage and becomes witness again. He faces audience the whole time. Earl remains on the floor. Lights shift. Soft spot on Ray. Esteban hangs near the stove. Conchalla goes to the bed and flops down on it. Henry approaches Earl. Both Henry and Conchalla are as drunk as the last time we saw them. Henry stops in front of Earl and sniffs the air.*]

HENRY: What stinks? What's that stink in here?

ESTEBAN: Menudo, Mr. Henry.

HENRY: Well turn that shit off! Smells like a goddamn Tijuana whorehouse in here. Turn it off! [*Esteban turns off the stove.*]

ESTEBAN: I was making it for Mr. Earl.

HENRY: What's a matter with "Mr. Earl"? What's he doing crawling around on my floor? [*To Earl.*] What're you doing down there?

EARL: I've lost track.

HENRY: Well get the hell up off my floor! This isn't some kind of a New York City crash pad or something. Have some respect. I've got a woman in the house, in case you didn't notice.

CONCHALLA: [*Calling out from bed.*] A woman! A woman in the house! [*Earl drags himself up from floor and just stands there.*]

HENRY: [*To Earl.*] What's the deal here anyway? You showing up outta the blue like this. What's the big idea?

EARL: Esteban told me it was an emergency.

HENRY: Emergency! He's a Mexican! Everything's an emergency with them.

EARL: He said you'd disappeared.

HENRY: Since when did you ever give two shits whether I disappeared or not? I haven't seen hide nor hair of you for— how long's it been now?

EARL: I forget.

HENRY: Yeah. Me too.

EARL: I wasn't—sure you wanted to see me.

HENRY: Oh, is that right? You weren't sure. Well, let's get clear about this then. Let's get this straight once and for all. Far as I'm concerned you never even existed! You were one big bad mistake! All right? Does that make any kind of sense to you at all?

EARL: Yeah. Yeah, that makes sense. That explains a whole lot.

HENRY: Good. Now you can clear on outta here because everything's just hunky-dory. Why in the hell does that stuff stink so bad? [*Henry crosses to Esteban. Conchalla giggles and turns over on the bed. To Esteban.*] What're you doin' here anyway? Why are you always here, stickin' yer nose into my business? Don't you have your own place? What is it about my place that's so damn attractive?

CONCHALLA: There is a woman! A woman in the house!

HENRY: [*To Conchalla.*] You pipe down! [*Conchalla rises from the bed and offers her arm out to Esteban.*]

CONCHALLA: I will take you to your trailer, Esteban. Come on. [*Esteban starts to cross to door but Conchalla intercepts him and throws her arms around him. Holding Esteban.*] I will take you there and bounce you on my knees! [*She squeezes Esteban in a bear hug and bounces him up and down. As she bounces Esteban.*] Wouldn't you like some bouncing? I will bounce you all night long until the sun explodes! Wouldn't you like that? Wouldn't you like some of that, Esteban?

HENRY: Knock it off! Knock it off! [*Conchalla stops bouncing Esteban and throws him backward onto the bed.*] He doesn't need any bouncing! [*Conchalla slowly approaches Esteban on bed.*]

CONCHALLA: He looks to me like a man who could use some bouncing. Look how flat he is.

HENRY: If there's any bouncing going on here I'll be the one in charge of it. [*Conchalla turns to Henry.*]

CONCHALLA: [*To Henry.*] Oh, you'll be the one?

HENRY: That's right. [*Now Conchalla approaches Henry, slow and seductive. Esteban gets up from bed and heads for the door.*]

CONCHALLA: [*Approaching Henry.*] You'll be the one in charge of bouncing? The Captain of Bouncing! I didn't know dead men were any good at bouncing. I thought their bouncing days were over.

HENRY: [*Appealing to Earl.*] There she goes again! She won't give it up. She goes around and around and around about it. She ate my fish, you know.

EARL: What?

HENRY: My fish I caught. She ate it. Raw! She's a barbarian! [*Henry crosses to bed and collapses on it. Pause as Earl just stands there, not knowing what to do with his father.*]

EARL: You need anything, Dad?

HENRY: [*Stays on bed.*] What!

EARL: You need something? You want me to get you something?

HENRY: Yeah—Most likely I do. Most likely I *need* something. I've got that feeling. What would it be? What would it be that I *need*? [*Pause. Earl moves closer to Henry, who remains crumpled on the bed. Earl stops.*]

EARL: You need a blanket or something?

HENRY: She's got the blanket! She takes everything. The blanket. The bottle. My fish.

EARL: Who is she, anyway?

HENRY: Who is she?

EARL: Yeah. I mean—I had no idea you were living with a woman.

HENRY: I'm not living with her! Don't be ridiculous. How could you live with something like that?

EARL: Well, whatever you call it.

HENRY: You don't call it living! [*Henry rolls over and sits up unsteadily. He stares at Earl.*] I don't suppose you've got a bottle, do ya?

EARL: No, I—

HENRY: Nah, you wouldn't have a bottle. You don't have a pot to piss in. [*Henry gets up and staggers toward refrigerator. He opens it and stares into it. Earl watches him. Staring into fridge.*] What're you doin' out here, anyway? Why'd you come all the way out here?

EARL: Esteban—He called me. He said you were in trouble or something. He said you'd disappeared. [*Henry laughs and slams refrigerator shut. Turns to Earl.*]

HENRY: Disappeared! Disappeared?

EARL: Yeah. That's what he said.

HENRY: [*Staggers toward Earl.*] Have you ever known anybody who's disappeared? Huh? [*He stops.*] Just—vanished?

EARL: No—

HENRY: No. That's not possible is it? Is that a possible thing for a human being? Just—disappear?

EARL: I don't know. I mean, I guess there have been—

HENRY: What?

EARL: Cases.

HENRY: Disappearing cases?

EARL: Yeah. [*Henry staggers closer to Earl and stops.*]

HENRY: Are you—Are you seeing me, right now?

EARL: What?

HENRY: Are you seeing me; perceiving me as we speak?

EARL: Well, yeah—Sure.

HENRY: You're sure?

EARL: Yeah. Why?

HENRY: You're convinced that I'm standing here before you? That I'm an actuality in this world?

EARL: Yeah.

HENRY: What's giving you that impression?

EARL: What?

HENRY: That I'm here. That I'm real? What's convincing you of that?

EARL: I—I recognize you.

HENRY: You do?

EARL: Yeah.

HENRY: What do you recognize? What is it?

EARL: I remember—

HENRY: What?

EARL: Your voice. Your eyes. The—smell.

HENRY: The smell? What smell?

EARL: That—that—

HENRY: Booze?

EARL: No.

HENRY: What, then?

EARL: Some—some—scent of you.

HENRY: A scent? You mean like a dog or something?

EARL: No—[*Suddenly Henry throws his arms around Earl and squeezes him in a bear hug. Earl panics but can't get out of it.*]

HENRY: [*Squeezing Earl.*] You mean like a dog, don't ya? Like a mad dog?

EARL: [*Struggling.*] No! Let go a me for God's sake!

HENRY: [*Still squeezing Earl in his grip.*] Like a dead man! Is that what you think? You ever known a dead man with a grip like this? [*Earl finally breaks free and shoves Henry back. They stand apart.*]

HENRY: You shouldn't take it personal.

EARL: That woman—

HENRY: Yeah. She's somethin', huh? Conchalla Lupina. Ever seen anything like her?

EARL: No—No, I never did.

HENRY: She'd scare the pants off a natural man. You probably couldn't handle a woman like that.

EARL: No, probably not. Where'd you meet her, anyway?

HENRY: Where'd I meet her? Where do ya suppose I'd meet her?

EARL: I have no idea. [*Henry begins to slowly approach Earl. At the same time, the door swings open and Conchalla is standing there watching. Henry's back is to her, but Earl can see her in the doorway. She takes sips from a bottle of tequila.*]

HENRY: [*As he moves to Earl.*] I was—"obliterated," as they say. Absolutely sloshed. Been in and outta that drunk tank down there for over a month. This time though—I woke up—she was on top a me. [*Laughs.*] She had me straddled!

EARL: [*Trying to end the story.*] All right, all right!

CONCHALLA: [*Giggles in doorway.*] He couldn't resist me! I was too much woman! [*Henry doesn't look back to Conchalla but keeps his focus on Earl. Earl backs away.*]

HENRY: I couldn't resist. It's true. There she was—big as day!

EARL: I—I don't really wanna hear about it, okay? [*Conchalla enters room and closes door behind her. She keeps sipping from bottle and smiling at Earl.*]

HENRY: Big as the damn Sangre de Cristo mountains! Right on top a me. What could I do?

CONCHALLA: He was whimpering when they threw him in. Hunched up in a corner, whining like a puppy.

HENRY: I wasn't whimpering. I had the shakes. Cold.

CONCHALLA: He was whimpering.

HENRY: [*Approaching Earl.*] Huddled up—trying to get some warmth. Just trying to find some warmth—that's all.

CONCHALLA: I gave him warmth.

EARL: [*Trying to escape them.*] That's enough!

CONCHALLA: I gave him so much warmth, he passed out. He couldn't take my warmth! [*Conchalla giggles as she and Henry close in on Earl.*]

HENRY: I could take it. I could take it.

CONCHALLA: When I dismounted him, his heart stopped. His breath. Nothing was moving.

EARL: I don't wanna hear any more of this! I don't wanna hear any more! All right? Stop telling me about this! Just stop telling me about all this! [*Henry and Conchalla stop suddenly. Henry notices Conchalla's bottle and approaches her, trying to get a hit off it, but she hides it behind her back. After pause.*] Look—for some strange reason or other, I still remember my mother, okay?

HENRY: Your mother?

EARL: Yeah. Yeah, that's right. My mother. I can still—picture her. I can—see her. I can—

HENRY: Your mother.

EARL: She was always—

HENRY: What?

EARL: Faithful. She was always faithful. No matter what. I remember her now. I remember her on her hands and knees.

HENRY: Your mother. That little shit. [*Conchalla giggles, drinks, goes to bed and flops down on it.*] Another traitor. Locked me out of my own house! That's what she did. Locked me out!

EARL: I remember that too.

HENRY: You remember nothin'! Your "mother." Wasn't for her, I wouldn't be in this mess I'm in right now. This whole— situation!

EARL: How is she to blame for that?

HENRY: She caused me to leave!! She caused me to pack on outta there! What'd'ya think? You think I wanted to wander around this Christless country for twenty some years like a refugee? Like some miserable fuckin' exile? Huh? You think I wanted that? She did that to me! She banished me! She turned me out!

EARL: You broke the place up. You smashed all the windows!

HENRY: SHE LOCKED ME OUT!!! [*Henry collapses, grabs onto the upstage chair and crashes to his knees. Earl moves toward him, but Conchalla stops him.*]

CONCHALLA: Don't touch him!

HENRY: [*On his knees, clutching chair.*] She locked me out— that's what she did to me. Locked me out completely.

CONCHALLA: Now he will start to crumble—to whimper. The same. Always the same.

EARL: Dad? You want a doctor or something? You wanna go to the hospital? [*Conchalla laughs and drinks from bottle.*]

CONCHALLA: The hospital! He is way beyond the hospital! [*Conchalla grabs Henry by the chest with tremendous force and lifts him up to the table. She lays him out on his back on the table as Earl watches helplessly.*]

EARL: What the hell're you doing to him! Haven't you done enough damage already? [*Conchalla giggles and strokes Henry's hair gently. Then she lifts his head and starts pouring the tequila into his mouth very gently, like medicine. Henry gurgles.*]

CONCHALLA: Damage? I have done no damage. I am just— watching out for the dead. Do you know how much trouble that is? Watching—always watching? It takes a lot of time. A lot of patience.

EARL: Stop it! Stop giving him that!! [*Earl lunges toward Conchalla, trying to grab the bottle away from her, but she lets out a blood-curdling scream and freezes Earl in his tracks. She giggles. She strokes Henry's face very gently.*]

CONCHALLA: I will show you your father. You see him now? You see how he looks to me. Helpless. Hoping. Dreaming. Wishing for death. Wishing for some way out. [*Stroking Henry's head.*] It takes courage, no? I gave him courage. A drowned man. He comes up for air. He gasps—[*Conchalla keeps pouring tequila down Henry as she straddles him. Stroking Henry's head.*] Now he begins to go back home. Now—he begins to return. You will see. He remembers now.

HENRY: [*Spitting to get his throat clear.*] I remember—The day I died—She was on the floor.

CONCHALLA: [*Gently.*] Now, he sees. [*Henry sits up on table with Conchalla supporting him and gently stroking his head. Earl watches.*]

HENRY: I remember the floor—was yellow—I can see the floor—and—her blood—her blood was smeared across it. I thought I'd killed her—but it was me. It was me I killed. [*Conchalla kisses Henry lightly on the forehead and helps him off the table. Henry stands there, looking out.*] I can see her eyes—peering up at me. Her swollen eyes. She just—stays there, under the sink. Silent. Balled up like an animal. Nothing moving but her eyes. She sees me. She knows. I can tell she knows. She sees me dying! Right there in front of her. She watches me pass away! There's nothing she can do. And then—there's this flash of grief—from her. Grief! Why would she grieve for me? [*Earl heads for the door.*]

EARL: I can't listen to this anymore! [*Conchalla moves fast in front of Earl and stops him.*]

CONCHALLA: [*To Earl.*] You watch.

HENRY: I ran out into the yard and I remember—I remember this—death. I remember it now—Cut off. Everything—far away. Birds. Trees. Sky. Removed! Everything—out beyond reach. And I ran. I ran to the car and I drove. I drove for days with the windows wide open. The wind beating across my eyes—my face. I had no map. No destination. I just—drove. [*Conchalla begins humming a death song and sways from side to side. She moves to Henry and hands him the bottle. Henry takes it and drinks. To Earl.*] You could've stopped me then but you didn't.

EARL: What? What're you talking about? [*Henry turns with bottle and moves toward Earl but trying more to get to the bed. Earl backs away from him. Conchalla continues to sway and hum her song.*]

HENRY: [*To Earl.*] You were there. You were there watching the whole time. I remember your beady eyes peering out at me from the hallway. You saw the whole thing.

EARL: I don't know what you're talking about!

HENRY: You saw! I looked straight at you! You looked straight back. Your mother was screaming the whole time!

EARL: No!! I was never there. I was never there for that!

HENRY: You coulda stopped me but you didn't. [*Henry almost loses his balance and crashes, but he staggers to the bed and goes down on top of it.*]

EARL: I couldn't. I–I–I was scared. I was–just–too–scared.

HENRY: You were scared! A what? A me? You were scared of a dead man? [*Henry takes a last giant pull on the bottle, then lies back and dies quietly. Conchalla stops humming her song. She moves to Henry and covers him with the blanket. She turns to Earl.*]

CONCHALLA: [*To Earl.*] The body–it stays. For three whole days no one must touch him. Not you. No one. You are the keeper. You watch now. [*Conchalla exits. Pause. Earl moves to bed and sits down next to Henry's corpse, facing directly out to audience. Pause. Ray turns to Earl but stays in his spot of light. Earl stares straight out.*]

RAY: Well, you know me, Earl–I was never one to live in the past. That never was my deal. You know–You remember how I was.

EARL: Yeah. Yeah, right. I remember. [*Lights fade slowly to black.*]

Eyes for Consuela

From the story "The Blue Bouquet" by Octavio Paz

Eyes for Consuela was first produced by Manhattan Theatre Club (Lynne Meadow, Artistic Director; Barry Grove, Managing Director), New York, on April 14, 1998, with the following cast:

VIEJO	Jose Perez
CONSUELA	Tanya Gingerich
HENRY	David Straithairn
AMADO	Daniel Faraldo
GUITARIST	Josué Pérez

Directed by Terry Kinney
Designed by Santo Loquasto
Costumes by Walt Spangler
Lighting by Jennifer Tipton
Music direction and sound by Rob Milburn
Original music by Josué Pérez
Choreography by Peter Pucci
Fight direction by Rick Sordelet
Production stage managed by Ruth Kreshka

Act One

Scene 1

In darkness a guitar is heard, in the Mexican corrido ballad style; slow and haunting. Night sky emerges in background cyclorama: stars, sliver moon, silhouetting a lush jungle fringe of palms, tamarinds and snaking vines. This border fringe of jungle runs from extreme down right in an arc and recedes into extreme upper left. Sounds of insects, jungle frogs and faint animal cries overlay guitar music. Moonlight keeps filling the space revealing a cheap two-story village boardinghouse, extreme down left. The corner of the boardinghouse juts out toward the audience like the prow of a ship. The ground floor has a recessed plank wood porch with no railings, open on three sides. A single black fan turns very slowly in the center, hung from the low floor of the second story, which comprises the roof of the porch. The porch abuts a faded blue adobe wall, patched and crumbling around the edges, with two thick-silled open windows, barred in black iron; an ancient oak plank door in the center. Faint yellow candlelight leaks from the windows. This lower story is the quarters of the boardinghouse owner, Viejo, a wizened old man in his seventies; beard, sombrero, baggy pants and jacket, bare feet, a gnarled walking stick and a black eye patch. He sits on the porch in an old rocking chair and from the opening moments he has been <u>slowly rocking</u>, marking a long tempo with the music as he faces the audience directly.

A rickety set of exterior stairs with a railing leads from the porch to a small landing on the second story. The stairs look like they've been slapped on to the stage right side of the structure. The second story is composed of open "walls" except for the back wall, which is faded pink adobe; plank wood floor and some implication of a sheet metal roof while still allowing light to pass through. Another black fan hangs from the center rafter of the ceiling, barely turning. A hammock strung between rafters, stage left of the room at an angle. A middle-aged gringo man, Henry, is asleep in the hammock with a mosquito net thrown over him. He is naked except for white boxer shorts. A small round table set against the back wall, center under a cracked mirror. A large clay pitcher of water and a washing bowl, along with a kerosene lantern sit on the table. A simple straight-backed chair beside the table with a towel thrown across the back. Henry's clothes are laid out neatly on the seat of the chair. Shoes and a suitcase on the floor. There are no other furnishings. The moonlight has not yet quite filled this space, so everything remains in silhouette.

The open stage floor space between the boardinghouse and the jungle fringe is packed in a reddish clay soil implying a roadway that leads from this tiny village junction off into nowhere up left. A young Mexican girl, Consuela, emerges from the jungle into the very center of the dirt road. Her skin is pale white and ghostly; jet-black long hair and red lips. She wears black and around her waist is a belt with long leather thongs that shift with her movement like a skirt. Blue eyeballs are attached to the end of each thong. She moves slowly with the guitar; looking from one end of the roadway to the other. Viejo keeps rocking, staring out at audience and not acknowledging her presence. Consuela is in a world of her own. Her movements seem to belong to some strange dream ritual; very slow and full of yearning.

Moonlight falls on Henry, still asleep as the guitar, dance and rocking of Viejo continue. Suddenly Henry bolts in the hammock and emits a sharp cry, as though reacting to a nightmare. Guitar stops. Viejo stops rocking. Consuela freezes. Pause. Insects and jungle sounds continue. Henry clamors up out of the hammock, struggling to free himself from mosquito netting and eject himself from the hammock. Consuela turns abruptly and darts off upstage, disappearing into the jungle. Henry gets to his feet and just stands there for a second, drenched in sweat. Viejo lights a cigarette. Henry crosses down to the very corner of the second story, right above Viejo, and looks out at the roadway, as though looking from a window. Pause. Viejo starts rocking again. Henry crosses back to the center of the room. Stops. Breathing deeply, as though trying to recover from some frightening vision. He wipes the sweat from his neck and face. He crosses to the pitcher of water on the table; pours some water into the basin; takes the towel from the chair; soaks it in the water, then wipes his face, neck, chest and arms.

HENRY: It's me. It's me. It *is* me. Me and my body. Here we are. Back together again. [*He soaks the towel again and wipes his legs, then throws the wet towel in a corner. He stops again and just stands there as though listening for something; as though waiting for something to emerge. Viejo keeps rocking and smokes. Henry breaks out of his stillness and moves to his clothes on the chair. Henry shakes his shirt out, checking for scorpions and bugs, and then puts it on.*] No bugs. No bugs. No biting. No stinging. No—pinching. [*He shakes out his pants.*] No critters. Good. [*He shakes out his shoes. When he's dressed he exits the second story to the landing.*] It's me. Here we are. We're going outside now. Here we go. [*Henry descends the stairs so that he arrives right beside Viejo on the porch level. Viejo stops rocking. He smokes and turns slowly to Henry.*]

VIEJO: It's late, my friend.

HENRY: Yes.

VIEJO: [*Starts rocking again.*] Ungodly hour.

HENRY: I was having—uh—Woke up in a sweat.

VIEJO: [*Chuckles.*] Must be a woman.

HENRY: A woman? No, uh—I don't know what it was. Just woke up ringing wet.

VIEJO: The jungle is singing.

HENRY: Yes. It is. Seems loud tonight.

VIEJO: [*Chuckles.*] Gringos—sometimes they don't understand these sounds down here.

HENRY: No, it wasn't that. I'm used to that by now. I don't know what it was. Some nightmare. [*Henry moves out toward middle of road.*]

VIEJO: Where are you going now, my friend?

HENRY: [*Stops.*] Just—take a walk. Too hot to sleep.

VIEJO: Everything is closed. No streetlights down here. They've been promising us streetlights since the Revolution.

HENRY: Yes—

VIEJO: You better stay put.

HENRY: No—I'm just going to take a stroll. I need to move.

VIEJO: You don't know what's out there, my friend.

HENRY: Well—I won't be long.

VIEJO: Buena suerte, amigo. [*Henry begins to walk, upstage on the road, toward the jungle. Guitar music under. Jungle sounds continue. Viejo rocks slowly and smokes. Henry lights a cigarette and continues walking upstage, then turns to his left at jungle fringe and makes his way downstage, along the border of trees and vines; taking in the stars, moon and the night air. He stops, extreme down right, facing the audience. He speaks to the audience directly but has a woman in mind. Guitar, sounds and Viejo's rocking continues.*]

HENRY: [*To audience.*] No look—What was I supposed to do? What exactly did you have in mind when you moved up there? What could I do? You knew I couldn't live in that climate—that ridiculous cold. It's crazy. Inhuman. Humans crave the sun. That's always been true. Humans worship the sun. Besides—you'd left already. Years ago. That was clear. You'd—turned your back on me. So now—I'm here. I'm down here now. [*Henry continues walking, smoking. He moves downstage left, then turns in front of boardinghouse and heads upstage, describing a large circle. When he passes Viejo it's as though they are in different worlds, making no acknowledgment of each other. Viejo keeps rocking. Guitar and sounds continue. Henry speaks again as he keeps walking upstage. To himself, as he walks.*] No, no it's not just stubborn. It's stupid. Insanity. Two people—Where are you now, for instance? Right now. I can't even imagine. I can't even picture you. We've grown that far apart. It's amazing. [*Henry keeps walking, circling downstage. When he reaches extreme down right again, he stops, facing audience. He speaks directly to audience. To audience.*] Me? Me? I'm surprised you ask. I'm down here, where I said I'd be. Where did you think? Where it's warm. Where they've never heard of ice. Steaming jungle. [*He turns and stares up at the stars.*] The stars have set up camp. That's right. That's exactly it. Can I be poetic? Why not? I'm completely alone. I'll be poetic. Right now, it's as though—it's as though the universe was a vast system of signs. Good. That's it. Yes. A conversation between giant beings. Yes. That's it. That's how it is. That's exactly how it is. I'm coming back to myself. After all this time. [*Henry starts walking again, same as before; turning upstage past the boardinghouse; turning left at the jungle and following the fringe downstage. A figure in white suddenly appears behind the jungle trees, upstage left, as Henry passes. The figure disappears just as fast behind the thick foliage. Henry stops, startled, sensing this presence, but isn't sure if he actually saw someone. The guitar stops. Viejo stops rocking. Pause. Jungle sounds continue. Henry listens, then continues walking again. He checks back over his shoulder as he walks but sees nothing lurking. He speaks to himself again as he walks downstage. Henry stops again. He turns toward the jungle. Pause.*] Is someone there? [*Pause.*] Is there someone out there? [*Henry starts walking again, repeating the same circular route. As he passes the jungle again, making his way downstage, a small thin man darts out of the jungle, behind Henry. This man, Amado, is dressed in the traditional white pajama outfit of the bracero. He wears a machete and knife in his belt, guaraches and a sombrero hangs on his back from a chin strap. Henry stops, turns and looks back at him. Amado stops. They stare at each other, then Henry turns and starts walking away from him. Amado follows him, getting closer. Henry stops again. Amado stops. Henry doesn't turn back to him. Henry starts walking again. Amado follows, getting closer yet. Henry stops again, not turning. Amado is very close now. Pause. Henry keeps his back to Amado as he speaks to him.*] Look—I'm—[*Henry makes a move as though to turn around and face Amado, but Amado quickly pulls his knife and holds it to Henry's back. Henry freezes.*]

AMADO: Don't move, mister, or I'll stick it in you.

HENRY: What do you want?

AMADO: Your eyes, mister.

HENRY: [*Pause.*] My eyes? What do you mean? What do you want with my eyes? Look—I've got some money. Not much, but it's something. I'll give you everything I have on me if you let me go. Don't kill me. Please.

AMADO: Don't be afraid, mister. I'm not going to kill you. I'm only going to take your eyes.

HENRY: [*Pause.*] My eyes? Why do you want my eyes?

AMADO: My woman—she has this whim. She's getting very greedy.

HENRY: For what?

AMADO: She wants a bouquet of blue eyes. And around here they're hard to find.

HENRY: Well my eyes won't help you, then. They're brown.

AMADO: [*Pressing knife harder into Henry's back.*] Don't try to fool me, mister. I know very well that your eyes are blue.

HENRY: No, please—Don't take the eyes of a fellow man. I'll give you something else. I have other valuables back at my room. Other—things.

AMADO: Don't play saint with me! "Fellow man"—Where does that come from? Turn around. [*Amado draws his machete now, very quickly.*] I want to see your face. Turn around! [*Henry slowly turns around, facing Amado, trembling slightly.*] Let me see your face. Strike a match. [*Henry takes out a small box of wooden matches, strikes one and holds the flame up by his face. Amado leans in closer and peers intently into Henry's eyes. Henry blinks.*] Don't blink! [*Amado reaches up quickly and pushes Henry's eyelids open. He keeps the machete pressed into Henry's belly. He keeps staring into Henry's eyes. The match burns Henry's finger, and he blows it out and drops it. Amado takes a step back but keeps the machete at the ready.*]

HENRY: Are you satisfied? They're not blue. They're brown.

AMADO: Pretty clever. Light another one. Let's see.

HENRY: I just showed you.

AMADO: Light another match! [*Henry lights another match and holds it up to his face. Amado suddenly grabs Henry's sleeve and yanks down on it.*] Kneel down! [*Henry kneels, holding the match near his face. If it happens to go out, he lights another one. His hands are shaking. Amado suddenly grabs Henry by the hair and jerks his head back. He very slowly raises the machete in an arc and lowers it until it is almost touching Henry's eyelid. Henry closes his eyes.*]

HENRY: Please—

AMADO: Keep them open. [*Henry slowly opens his eyes. The machete is very close. Amado peers into Henry's eyes again. A long pause where anything could happen. Then, suddenly, Amado releases Henry's hair, shoving him backward to the floor. Amado returns his machete to his belt.*] Pretty clever. You think you've fooled me, don't you?

HENRY: [*On ground.*] No. They're actually brown. They really are brown. You can see that for yourself.

AMADO: [*Pause.*] Where is this room of yours?

HENRY: Off the plaza. The corner.

AMADO: Stand up.

HENRY: Please, I—

AMADO: Stand up! And stop pleading like a goat. Act like a man. [*Henry slowly stands, brushing himself off. Amado draws his small knife.*] Give me a cigarette. [*Henry gives him one and lights it. His hands are still shaking.*] Stop shaking. You're not going to die. [*Pause. Amado smokes.*] Now. Take me there.

HENRY: To my room?

AMADO: Yes. Take me to it. Now. [*Henry turns slowly and walks toward boardinghouse. Amado comes up behind him and holds knife to his back. Viejo begins rocking again. Henry and Amado approach the porch and stop by Viejo, who acknowledges them and continues to rock slowly.*]

VIEJO: [*Rocking.*] Ah, you see? I tried to tell you.

HENRY: [*To Viejo.*] This man—

AMADO: [*To Viejo, knife to Henry's back.*] Where is his room?

VIEJO: [*Pointing toward Henry's room.*] Es allá.

AMADO: [*Nudging Henry with knife.*] Go. [*Henry moves to stairs and starts climbing them with Amado right behind.*]

HENRY: [*To Viejo as he climbs.*] This man is a bandit!

VIEJO: [*Chuckles; keeps rocking.*] What man isn't?

Scene Segue

Guitar comes in again and Consuela emerges from the jungle. Henry and Amado continue to ascend stairs and enter the second-floor room of the boardinghouse. They do not acknowledge the presence of Consuela. <u>Viejo keeps rocking</u> and smoking. Consuela flows toward the staircase with her head swept back, as though captured by the moon and stars. She hovers under the staircase, then reemerges and moves to the down center of the road. She looks up at the second-floor room, then darts back upstage and disappears into jungle again. Guitar fades. <u>Viejo keeps slowly rocking</u>.

Scene 2

Amado and Henry in the second-floor room.

AMADO: Light the lamp.

HENRY: Look—I'm just down here on a kind of—vacation. I don't—

AMADO: Be silent! Light the lamp. [*Henry lights kerosene lantern on small table. Light fills the pink adobe wall. Pause. Amado removes his sombrero, tosses it on chair, then moves toward Henry slowly, machete swinging at his side. Still with knife in his hand.*] I have no interest in you. I don't care why you're here or who you are. I only care about one thing. Just one. Making my woman happy. Right now, she is not happy. She is sad. Her sadness is my doing. It is my duty to change that.

[*Amado paces slowly, tapping knife on his leg. Henry stands still. Pause.*]

HENRY: I wish I could help you.

AMADO: Your wish is to run. To be far away. Don't lie to me.

HENRY: I just—don't understand.

AMADO: Sit down. By the lamp. Sit! [*Henry moves to chair by table; removes Amado's sombrero; isn't quite sure where to put it, so he sits in chair and places sombrero on his lap. The lamp flickers on Henry's face.*] Turn your face to the light. [*Henry does what he's told. Amado moves toward him with the knife.*] Open wide your eyes. [*Henry follows instructions. Amado moves closer and peers into Henry's eyes again. Pause.*]

HENRY: [*Eyes wide.*] Why can't you see they're not blue? They're not blue eyes. I don't know how many times you have to look. [*Pause as Amado keeps looking intensely into Henry's eyes with the knife held up. Then, suddenly, Amado turns away and paces the room again, leaving Henry sitting at table.*]

AMADO: [*Pacing.*] Do you have a woman?

HENRY: I—yes. Yes, I do.

AMADO: Only one?

HENRY: Yes. Of course.

AMADO: [*Laughs.*] "Of course!" Of course.

HENRY: My wife.

AMADO: Aah—How long? How long, your wife and you?

HENRY: You mean—together?

AMADO: Yes. Together. How long?

HENRY: Well—It's been off and on now for over twenty years.

AMADO: Off and on? Off and on. What does this mean, "Off and on"?

HENRY: We haven't exactly—seen things—eye to eye over the years.

AMADO: [*Whirling around toward Henry.*] Are you making fun of me?

HENRY: No. No, not at all. [*Pause. Amado starts pacing again.*]

AMADO: [*Pacing.*] And which way are you now? You and your wife. "Off" or "on"?

HENRY: We—We're separated now.

AMADO: Separated. Apart?

HENRY: Yes.

AMADO: Then—that's "off," no?

HENRY: Yes.

AMADO: And you—you're suffering from this? Your wife is suffering?

HENRY: Well—

AMADO: Be a man. You must know these things. You must know them by heart.

HENRY: Yes. Sometimes.

AMADO: Sometimes suffering? Sometimes not?

HENRY: Yes.

AMADO: It comes and goes, this suffering?

HENRY: Yes.

AMADO: Why is that?

HENRY: [*Pause.*] I—I don't know.

AMADO: You don't—wonder about it?

HENRY: What?

AMADO: This suffering! "Off and on." On and off. It doesn't puzzle you?

HENRY: I never—I never actually thought about it much.

AMADO: Ah, so you just suffer like a dog? A whipped dog.

HENRY: No, I—

AMADO: Tell the truth. What have you got to lose? [*Henry suddenly gets up fast and moves toward his suitcase.*]

HENRY: Look, I've got some things I could give you. Valuable things. They've been in my family a very long time.

AMADO: Sit back down! [*Pause. Henry stops. They just stare at each other, then Henry returns to the chair and sits. Viejo continues rocking.*] You—have nothing to give me—but your eyes.

HENRY: Why do you keep—

AMADO: I was a "mojado" once.

HENRY: [*Pause.*] What?

AMADO: A "mojado." A "wet." I wanted "things." "Valuable things." I swam the river in the dead of night. Dogs tried to eat me. Searchlights cut across my head. I ran for miles in the night. My lungs were screaming but my head kept dreaming of "things." "Valuable things."

HENRY: I see—

AMADO: And I got them too. Many "valuable things": Tennis shoes. T-shirts. Television.

HENRY: Yes.

AMADO: Radios. VCR. Refrigerator. Ford Mustang. I even got the biggest prize of all.

HENRY: What was that?

AMADO: A gringa! Yes. Blonde. Blue eyes. Very young. Joven y dura. She wanted me very badly. She wanted my darkness. I wanted her light. So—we married.

HENRY: That's—That's nice.

AMADO: Now, I was a citizen. A real American citizen, with papers. Legal. I could come and go without swimming the Bravo. Without shame.

HENRY: Where is she now? Your wife.

AMADO: Dallas, Texas. Home of the "Cowboys."

HENRY: You're—separated too?

AMADO: Apart. Yes. Like you.

HENRY: Did you have—children together?

AMADO: Yes. Two. I haven't seen them for five years.

HENRY: Why is that?

AMADO: Because, mister—What is your name?

HENRY: Henry. Henry—

AMADO: Because, Mr. Henry—my heart was bleeding.

HENRY: Your heart?

AMADO: Yes. It was bleeding wherever I went. In the street. At my job. Wherever I went I left a trail of blood. In bed with my gringa wife. The sheets were always red.

HENRY: Your—heart?

AMADO: Yes.

HENRY: It was actually—bleeding?

AMADO: It was bleeding for my homeland.

HENRY: Oh. Oh, well, that's different.

AMADO: But, most of all—Most of all it was bleeding for—Consuela.

HENRY: Consuela?

AMADO: Yes.

HENRY: Who is she?

AMADO: She is the one who needs your eyes.

HENRY: [*Stands suddenly.*] No! This is ridiculous! I don't have blue eyes! I've never had blue eyes! I will never have blue eyes in the future! I was not born a blue-eyed person! Why can't you understand that? It was never in the genes! I'm a brown-eyed person. Just like you. Look! [*Pause. Amado just stares at him.*]

AMADO: My eyes—are black. [*Henry begins to move, very tentatively, around the space. Amado allows him but keeps a close watch on his every move.*]

HENRY: [*Moving cautiously.*] Now, look—I can—I can empathize with your situation. Women can be very—persuasive in certain areas. Very—I mean a man can find himself doing things he never dreamed—Things he never imagined. And—suddenly you see that you're in—a pickle.

AMADO: A "pickle"? What is a "pickle"?

HENRY: A—conundrum. A dilemma. I mean—Take me, for instance—uh—I'm uh—having some difficulties myself. I mean, my situation might be very similar in some ways to your own.

AMADO: You have no idea about me.

HENRY: No—No I don't. It's true, but I can see certain—

AMADO: You have never seen me before in your life.

HENRY: No. No, I haven't.

AMADO: You will never see me again. After this.

HENRY: I—

AMADO: I have just appeared to you. Out of nowhere. [*Pause. Henry stands still. They stare at each other. <u>Viejo stops rocking</u>. Henry begins moving again.*]

HENRY: [*Pacing.*] I don't—I don't want any trouble. I—I came down here just to get away for a while. Just to—

AMADO: You have left your wife? [*Henry stops.*]

HENRY: [*Pause.*] Yes—Well, we both agreed it would be better to be apart.

AMADO: Better for who?

HENRY: For us both. It was mutual.

AMADO: You don't know your heart. [*Pause. Henry begins to pace again.*]

HENRY: [*Moving.*] No—I suppose that's true. I suppose you're right about that. I keep thinking—It's funny, you know—

AMADO: What is funny?

HENRY: I just realized—I mean, you know how you can be going along, kind of thinking everything is perfectly normal—perfectly sane—and—I—I keep having these little dialogues with her. Out loud.

AMADO: Your wife?

HENRY: Yes. These little running commentaries. As though she's right here with me. Right here now. I talk out loud to her. Argue with her. Reason with her. Out loud. To myself.

AMADO: But she is not here.

HENRY: No. She's not. That's what I'm trying to say. She's not here at all. She's somewhere else. And I—Well, that's what I was trying to say before—How there might be certain similarities in our predicament. I mean—I thought—What I thought was, that I would come down here to get away from her. Maybe that would help. Something—You know, I would be in a warm place. The sun on my back. Surrounded by parrots and—I might forget all about her. Find a new life.

AMADO: Parrots?

HENRY: Yes. You know—sounds. Tropical sounds. They would take me away. Spanish. Palm trees. Tequila. A whole new environment. It would distract me. I could start all over.

AMADO: Tequila? Do you have tequila?

HENRY: Yes. As a matter of fact, I do. I have some right here. Would you like some tequila?

AMADO: I would like some, yes. [*Henry goes to his bag and pulls out a bottle of tequila, half full. He gets a glass from the table and pours a drink.*]

HENRY: Good. That's good. I've been carrying it around with me. It was a gift. Unfortunately, I only have one glass. This hotel is not much on service.

AMADO: *You* take the glass.

HENRY: [*Offering glass to Amado.*] No, no please. I insist.

AMADO: You take the glass. I will take the bottle.

HENRY: [*Pause.*] Of course. [*Amado takes bottle and drinks from it. A long, thirsty drink. Henry watches, then sips from glass. Pause. Amado looks at label on bottle.*]

AMADO: [*Reading label.*] "Hornitos primero"! Muy bien. [*He toasts Henry with bottle.*] Hasta no verte, dios mío.

HENRY: [*Toasting.*] Yes. Cheers. This is uh—one thing I've learned to respect since I've been down here.

AMADO: What is that?

HENRY: Tequila. I've learned to sip it. [*Amado takes another long drink from bottle. Henry watches. Pause. Amado wipes his mouth with his sleeve then puts the cap back on bottle. He goes to chair and sits by table.*]

AMADO: So—Mr. Henry—you thought you could escape. [*Viego starts rocking again.*]

HENRY: Escape?

AMADO: Yes. You thought Mexico could hide you—from your-self.

HENRY: No, I—

AMADO: Mexico is very harsh on liars.

HENRY: I wasn't lying. I wasn't trying to hide. I simply came down here to—make a new start.

AMADO: It's too late for you.

HENRY: [*Pause.*] You don't know anything about me. You're in no position to say something like that.

AMADO: You're too old to start over. Same as me. Much too old.

HENRY: I'm not *that* old.

AMADO: We're both too old. All we can hope for now is to pay for our sins.

HENRY: Sins? Look—I'm not a Catholic, myself.

AMADO: No. But you *are* a sinner.

HENRY: [*Pause.*] I'm not going to get into this. I—I—I would like you to leave now. Please. [*Amado starts laughing and can't stop. Pause.*] I'll call the police!

AMADO: [*Laughing.*] Police!

HENRY: I will.

AMADO: [*Laughing.*] There is no phone!

HENRY: I'll have the old man bring them then.

AMADO: [*Laughing.*] There is no police! No phone! [*He stops laughing and grins at Henry.*] Now that's—a "pickle." [*Viejo stops rocking. Long pause. Amado drinks. Henry watches.*]

HENRY: Did you—just happen to see me, out there? I mean—were you waiting for me? Lurking? Was this just an accident? I just—happened to take a walk at the wrong time?

AMADO: I am always hunting for new eyes. [*Henry starts pacing again. Viejo starts rocking. Amado stays in chair.*]

HENRY: [*Pacing.*] This woman of yours—

AMADO: Yes.

HENRY: Why is she making you do this? I mean, why is she making this insane demand?

AMADO: She and I have been lovers since we were children. In the same pueblo, we grew up.

HENRY: Lovers?

AMADO: Yes. Companions of the heart. From the very first moment we laid eyes on each other.

HENRY: How old were you—when this happened? When you first saw each other.

AMADO: She was five. I was seven.

HENRY: And—you became lovers? At that age?

AMADO: Yes.

HENRY: Not—I mean—did you have—

AMADO: Your mind is American. Like a scorpion. Love is out-side your language. You have lost this word.

HENRY: No—I mean—it's unusual—so young.

AMADO: We had two children before I turned eighteen.

HENRY: Two? So—this other family—with the woman in Dal-las—you have two wives, then? [*Pause. Amado stands slowly. He smiles kindly at Henry.*]

AMADO: [*Motioning to chair.*] Mr. Henry, please—come and sit.

HENRY: No, I'm—It's all very fascinating, but I'd really like to be left alone now, if you don't mind.

AMADO: [*Repeating gesture to chair.*] Please. [*Pause, then Henry goes to chair and sits. Amado moves away from him and begins telling his story. Moving.*] Every year there was a fiesta in our pueblo. The Fiesta of Independence. On this day I would always love to drink *sotol* and shoot my pistol into the sky. Every year on this day I would do this. And Consuela would dance. [*Guitar comes in. Consuela appears from jungle and begins to move along the fringe. Continuing.*] She would dance as though she were being carried away by the angels. There was a happiness in my heart I have never known the likeness of since that time. Then, on this one day, many years ago—the last time I took part in our fiesta—I fired my pistol deep into the blue sky. I was wild with the feeling of freedom and my love for Consuela. The liquor rushed through my blood like boiling water. But one of my bullets must have hit something and bounced off. It struck Consuela's father, Don Morello, in the eye. He fell in the street and we all rushed to him, not knowing at first what had happened. He just fell over on his face as though it might have been a stroke or heart attack. When we rolled him over and I saw his eye gushing with blood, I knew it was my bullet that had caused this. I saw Consuela's face quivering. She was kneeling right across from me. Both of us staring at each other across the chest of her father. He was still alive. His chest rising and falling between us. In that moment, my life was changed. This one careless accident of my wildness turned everything upside down. He was taken far away to the hospital in Matamoros. They told us they could save his life but not his eye. I knew then the only honorable thing would be for me to pay his hospital bill. But I had no money. I had no money at all. I had spent it all on bullets for my pistol. So I kissed Consuela and swam the river to the United States, in order to find work. [*Consuela vanishes into jungle. Guitar fades. Viejo continues rocking.*]

HENRY: Then how—how could you take up with another woman?

AMADO: I kept returning—bringing what little money I'd earned each time. Each time the dogs would chase me. I would go to jail. They would throw me back into Mexico. I would go to Consuela and the children, then swim the river, back to America.

HENRY: Why go back?

AMADO: To work, Mr. Henry. There is no work in Mexico. Poverty is our prison.

HENRY: So, this other woman—the blonde woman was just—a way of—staying in America?

AMADO: A way of paying off my debt.

HENRY: It seems—I don't know—like you piled an awful lot of trouble on yourself.

AMADO: Trouble follows trouble.

HENRY: So then—Consuela's father lived, I take it?

AMADO: Oh, yes. He is very much alive.

HENRY: But she still blamed you for his accident?

AMADO: No. She has never blamed me for anything.

HENRY: Then—why—why does she ask you to do this savage thing?

AMADO: She simply woke up one morning with this idea in her head. This whim. It came to her in a dream, she said.

HENRY: And you didn't—I mean—have you actually cut the eyes out of other men?

AMADO: Yes. I have.

HENRY: How many?

AMADO: Sixteen.

HENRY: [*Stands suddenly.*] Sixteen men!

AMADO: Yes.

HENRY: You've cut their eyes out?

AMADO: Yes, of course.

HENRY: [*Staggers.*] That's—that's just—beyond my comprehension. I don't—how could you possibly do such a thing to another human being?

AMADO: Because, Mr. Henry, each time I present these gifts to Consuela she will smile slightly. The corners of her mouth will break and tremble. She will look up at me and touch me with her eyes. These are the only moments when she smiles. I live for these moments.

HENRY: How can she ask you to do this over and over? Doesn't she have any sense of the suffering she's causing? [*Amado laughs and doesn't stop. Long pause as Henry just watches him.*] What in God's name? Are you completely out of your mind? Is that it? Insane? [*Amado suddenly stops laughing. Viejo stops rocking. Amado lunges at Henry, grabs him by the chest and throws him to the ground with surprising ferocity. He gets on top of Henry's chest, pins his head to the ground and draws his knife, holding it above Henry's eyes. Screaming.*] Nooo!! Oh my God—My God! Please don't do this! Please! I beg of you. [*Pause. Amado freezes with the knife poised over Henry's eyes.*]

AMADO: [*Straddling Henry.*] You believe I am crazy? Is that what you believe?

HENRY: No—I—

AMADO: You believe I am a madman just out wandering the streets?

HENRY: No! No, I don't. I just—

AMADO: You believe nothing!

HENRY: I'm just—

AMADO: You think the happiness of my woman is not important?

HENRY: No, I didn't say that.

AMADO: You believe her smile is not like the morning sun rising in my heart?

HENRY: No. Please—

AMADO: You believe that love comes cheaply? That it costs nothing at all!

HENRY: No!

AMADO: You believe nothing. Nada! [*Amado pushes off Henry and stands, leaving Henry on floor. Pause. Amado takes a few steps away from Henry, turns his back on him and takes another long drink from the bottle.*]

HENRY: [*Still on floor.*] I was simply trying to say that—[*Amado turns abruptly back to Henry and kicks him in the ribs.*]

AMADO: You believe in shit! [*Long pause. Amado crosses to table and sits in chair, drinks. He picks his ears with his knife, wiping* *the wax on his pants leg. <u>Viejo begins to rock again slowly</u>. Henry rises painfully on one elbow, nursing his ribs.*]

HENRY: [*From floor.*] I didn't mean to insult you. I'm sorry. [*Amado is silent; keeps picking his ears. Pause. <u>Viejo keeps rocking</u>.*] I'm not accustomed to the uh—the ways—I mean the customs in some of these small villages. I mean, I keep forgetting I'm not in a big city. Veracruz or—Acapulco or something. I know—[*Pause. Silence from Amado. Henry tries to sit up with some difficulty.*] I certainly didn't mean to belittle your feelings for your wife. That wasn't my intention at all. I mean—I can remember, myself, when I—when those feelings were alive in me. It was—it was pure heaven to see the joy on my wife's face sometimes. Over the simplest things. A cup of coffee. The morning mail. The *Sunday Times*. Simple things like that. You know—So I'm—completely in sympathy with you there. I know what that's like. Believe me. [*Pause. Silence from Amado, who keeps picking his ears and drinking. Henry tries to find a comfortable position on floor. <u>Viejo keeps rocking</u>.*] I don't know why—I mean I don't understand how that all could have left me. You know—I don't know what happened exactly. How it changed. One day—it was—just gone. She became cold. Indifferent. As soon as—the children— I mean, as soon as she became pregnant, really. I couldn't believe it.

AMADO: [*Picking his ears.*] You're not going to weep are you, Mr. Henry?

HENRY: No. No, I don't think so.

AMADO: Good. No weeping.

HENRY: I'm just—saying—I feel as though we have—

AMADO: We have nothing in common. [*Pause. Viejo keeps rocking.*]

HENRY: It just—calls something up in me—what you said, about your wife. I mean—I start remembering—it's amazing.

AMADO: What is amazing?

HENRY: How things change. I was like—an outsider. Suddenly. Suddenly a complete stranger. I would walk into a room with her and she would turn her back on me. She would never speak. We would go days without talking. Not a word between us. I would lie beside her in bed, staring at the ceiling while she pretended to be asleep. I knew she was awake. I could tell by her breathing. But she wouldn't speak. I wanted to touch her but I—couldn't raise my arm. I would lie frozen there in silence, staring at the ceiling until finally her breathing changed and she dropped off into dreaming. As though dying. Something in me began to grieve. Grief. Just like mourning for the dead. It went on for years. [*Pause.*] By now we'd grown hard against each other. Contempt. We despised each other's presence. We were enemies of the heart.

AMADO: [*Pause.*] Why do you feel the need to tell me this? Why do you think I would be interested?

HENRY: I don't know. It just—came up.

AMADO: You and your unhappy wife—lying in bed. Staring at the ceiling. Why do you think this is something I should know?

HENRY: I—don't know. I thought it was similar in some way.

AMADO: Similar?

HENRY: Yes—uh—Do you think uh—Do you think it might be possible for me to meet this—Consuela?

AMADO: [*Laughs.*] You?

HENRY: Yes. I would like to meet her.

AMADO: Why you?

HENRY: I would like to—ask her something.

AMADO: [*Sneers.*] You would like to show her your eyes. Try to convince her, like me, that they are brown.

HENRY: No. I would just like to see her. [*Pause. Amado stares at him.*]

AMADO: Give me a cigarette.

HENRY: Sure. [*Henry fishes for cigarettes; offers one out to Amado.*]

AMADO: Give me the whole pack. [*Henry hands him the pack. Amado takes it and draws out a cigarette.*] Give me your matches. [*Henry lights a match for him.*] Not a light. Give me all your matches. [*Henry blows out match and hands him the whole box. Amado lights his cigarette. Pause. Amado smokes.*] Do *you* want a cigarette?

HENRY: No, thanks. I'm fine.

AMADO: Would you like more tequila?

HENRY: No. Thank you very much. [*Pause. Amado smokes and stares at Henry. Henry squirms under his scrutiny.*]

AMADO: [*Grins.*] You would like to meet Consuela?

HENRY: Yes—Yes, I would.

AMADO: If you met Consuela, you would not be able to speak. She would take your breath away.

HENRY: I—imagine her to be very beautiful.

AMADO: She has grown younger as I grow old.

HENRY: Yes—I know that feeling.

AMADO: It's not a feeling. It is true.

HENRY: [*Pause.*] So, do you think it might be possible?

AMADO: What.

HENRY: To meet her.

AMADO: [*Laughs.*] What is it you want to ask her?

HENRY: I would like to ask her—where her sadness comes from. This kind of sadness that can cause such—[*Pause. Viejo stops rocking.*]

AMADO: I have told you. Her sadness comes from me.

HENRY: Yes, but why? You said she's never blamed you—

AMADO: In America everything is easy. Food is easy. The roads are paved like silk. Money is easy. Sex. Movies. Drugs. It becomes easy to forget yourself. To eat candy. To move farther and farther and farther away from your heart. Until one day, Mr. Henry, you discover you are swimming alone at night in a deep black sea. There is no shore. No light. No sound. You are worse than alone. You are removed from life itself.

HENRY: This has nothing to do with—

AMADO: Your heart comes back to you, in this moment. It comes back screaming like a child at birth. You listen. Now—You *must* listen. You hear what it's screaming for. You hear it very clearly.

HENRY: I don't—

AMADO: It is crying out to be rejoined, Mr. Henry. To be reconnected to the body. To be remembered by its long lost partner. This is why Consuela has suffered. This is why I have returned to Mexico. And this is why I must take your eyes.

HENRY: [*Stands abruptly, screaming.*] Noooo! No, no, no, no, no! It makes no sense! It absolutely makes no sense! This whole thing is a complete accident. Why me? You don't even know me. I've never done anything to you!

AMADO: You have blue eyes.

HENRY: I DON'T HAVE BLUE EYES!! Why can't you get that through your head? Look, we have got to get something settled here. This is a total misunderstanding. I've told you— I would be more than happy to donate some very valuable items here. I have some family heirlooms that I have never even dreamed of parting with—

AMADO: You can't buy me, Mr. Henry.

HENRY: I'm not trying to buy you! I'm trying to buy—my life! [*Pause. Viejo begins rocking again. Amado is silent.*] Besides, what's she going to say? Consuela—when you bring her brown eyes instead of blue? How are you going to explain that? What are you going to do? Say you made a mistake? She's not going to be very happy, is she? I mean—if the whole point of this thing is to make her happy—I just— [*Henry begins pacing again. Viejo keeps rocking.*]

AMADO: Maybe you should sleep, Mr. Henry.

HENRY: Sleep! Sleep? Are you out of your mind? How can I sleep when there's a maniac in my room?

AMADO: I promise to do nothing until sunrise.

HENRY: Oh—Oh, well that's reassuring! That ought to send me right off into dreamland! I'll just lay there with peaceful visions of myself with my eyes gouged out, staggering into sixteen other blind men. What—what—What's become of these men, anyway? Where are they now?

AMADO: I have not followed them.

HENRY: You just cut their eyes out and left them to their own devices?

AMADO: I am not the inventor of cruelty, Mr. Henry.

HENRY: Aaah! Aha! So at least you admit it! At least you recognize the bestiality of it.

AMADO: I recognize the beast in everything. [*Pause. Viejo keeps rocking.*]

HENRY: You must be—You must be a very desperate man. I thought *I* was in trouble. I mean, I thought I had some difficulties with women but—this—This is just incredible. I mean, do you realize the power that she has over you? You've become her slave. Her lackey.

AMADO: You need sleep, Mr. Henry.

HENRY: Stop saying that! I don't need sleep! And even if I did need sleep I couldn't sleep. Even before this happened I couldn't sleep.

AMADO: Maybe—you are ill.

HENRY: Maybe I am. Maybe that's it. It's very possible.

AMADO: Maybe—too much tequila.

HENRY: No. No, I don't drink that much. Just a nightcap now and then.

AMADO: Maybe—the moon.

HENRY: What? The moon? What's the moon got to do with it?

AMADO: Maybe you are on the edge of seeing something.

HENRY: [*Pause.*] What?

AMADO: Sometimes, when things are bad like this—shaking, trembling, talking to someone who's not there—it is a sign.

HENRY: A sign of what? [*Pause. Viejo keeps rocking. Amado is silent.*]

AMADO: I, myself, am very tired. Muy cansado.

HENRY: A sign of what? Answer me!

AMADO: Would you mind, Mr. Henry, if I use your hammock for a while? [*Amado moves slowly toward hammock weaving slightly from the tequila.*]

HENRY: My hammock? No—sure—be my guest. "Mi casa es su casa!"

AMADO: Muchísimas gracias. [*Amado climbs into hammock, keeping bottle of tequila clutched to his chest. Henry watches him in amazement.*]

HENRY: [*Pause.*] You're going to—go to sleep now? Is that it? Right in the middle of all this, you're going to go to sleep in my hammock?

AMADO: I am as tired as the burro at the top of the mountain.

HENRY: You're going to go to sleep? How can you possibly sleep? How can a man who's done the things you've done possibly fall asleep? I can't sleep and I haven't done anything nearly as terrible as what you've done.

AMADO: I will dream of Consuela. What will you dream of, Mr. Henry? [*Henry moves away from him slowly, extreme down right, facing out toward audience. Amado keeps slowly swinging in hammock. Lights begin to fade almost imperceptibly as Henry speaks directly to audience but as though to his woman.*]

HENRY: [*Softly, to audience.*] Maybe—it's possible—I've made a mistake coming down here. Maybe, it's just possible. I mean—the heat of the moment—all that accumulation of misunderstanding. All those—bitter moments—piling up. Maybe—nothing—maybe nothing was seen. [*Pause.*] Nothing. [*Pause.*] Where are you now? [*Pause.*] Where are you right now? [*Pause.*] I can't—see you. [*Guitar comes in. Lights dimming. Consuela emerges and dances into the street. Henry does not see her. Viejo does not see her. Lights keep fading so that just the moonlight is cast on the dancing figure of Consuela. Moon fades to black. Guitar goes out.*]

Act Two

Morning. Sounds of rooster and turkeys gobbling mingled with jungle sounds. Light rises on Viejo asleep in rocker; head slumped into his chest. He awakens slowly to the sounds and the morning light. He rises and goes into the ground-floor room, closing door behind him and leaving the empty rocker moving on its own.

Upstairs the rising light reveals Amado asleep on his back in the hammock. The hammock swinging slightly with the empty rocker below. Henry is curled up asleep in the middle of the floor with a jacket wrapped around him. The empty bottle of tequila rolls off Amado's stomach and hits the floor. Amado stays asleep. Henry wakes up with a jolt. He is wringing wet with sweat again; same as the opening of Act One. He seems completely disoriented for a second. He scrambles to his feet and repeats the same actions as opening Act One: he crosses downstage of the upper floor and looks out; crosses back to center of room; stares at Amado, still sleeping; Henry breathes deep and wipes the sweat from his neck and face; he crosses to pitcher of water, pours it into basin, soaks towel then wipes his chest, neck and face. He unbuckles his belt, drops his pants and begins wiping his legs. Amado wakes up in hammock to discover Henry standing there, pants around his ankles, wiping his legs with towel. Pause as Amado just observes Henry's actions from hammock.

AMADO: Have you—had an accident, Mr. Henry? [*Henry quickly pulls his pants back up and buckles his belt. He continues wiping his neck and face with towel. Amado stays in hammock. Pause.*]

HENRY: I have to leave now. I have to—find a plane out of here.

AMADO: [*Laughing.*] A plane?

HENRY: Yes. A plane. An aeroplane.

AMADO: You're going to return to your wife?

HENRY: I have to get back.

AMADO: But, Mr. Henry—what if she has found someone else?

HENRY: [*Quickly turning to him, pause.*] What? No. How could you suggest such a thing. That's not—That's not possible.

AMADO: Anything is possible with a woman.

HENRY: She wouldn't—

AMADO: Why should she be faithful? You have grown apart. Separate.

HENRY: I don't want to discuss this! It's got nothing to do with you anyway. I'm going back and that's all there is to it. Now—would you mind—just leaving? [*Pause. Henry moves to his suitcase, takes out a fresh shirt; shakes it, checking for scorpions, and starts putting it on. Amado watches him, then climbs out of hammock. He clutches his head with hangover pain; crosses to pitcher of water and dumps water over his head into basin, then wipes his head with towel.*]

AMADO: [*Drying his head.*] You have had a change of heart?

HENRY: I'm not going to discuss it! I told you that. I think you should just—vamoose. Get lost. All right? Go away now. This has gone far enough.

AMADO: I thought you wanted to meet my woman, Mr. Henry. Last night, you said—

HENRY: That was last night. This is a brand-new morning here. This whole thing has just gotten completely out of hand. Way out of hand. I mean—what exactly are you doing here? I don't even know you. I don't *want* to know you. I didn't ask for this—to be tormented by a total stranger. I didn't come down here for that. I came down here for a little peace and quiet. Not torture! Not abuse. I'm a U.S. citizen, for Christ's sake! I mean—I've done nothing against you or your country. I'm a visitor! A tourist. I bring money into your country. Commerce! If it weren't for me and others like me, your country—Well, look—I just—I don't want to discuss it. The whole thing is ridiculous. I'm heading back and that's all there is to it. I need to find a taxi. If you'd be so kind as to try to help me find a taxi, I—well, I won't press any charges. Let's just leave it at that. [*Henry begins to pack his bag. Pause as Amado watches him.*]

AMADO: Where is your home, Mr. Henry? Where in America?

HENRY: [*Continues packing.*] My home? Well—my wife moved back—to Michigan. That's where she's from. Her mother is very sick and she felt she needed to go back up there. To be with her mother.

AMADO: Michigan?

HENRY: Yes.

AMADO: That is north?

HENRY: Yes. Very far north. Very cold. Freezing, in fact. They ice fish and run Ski-Doos all over the place. They think that's fun up there.

AMADO: You are not happy in Michigan?

HENRY: No. Not particularly. No, I'm not.

AMADO: That is not where you are from? Michigan?

HENRY: No.

AMADO: Where is *your* home, then, Mr. Henry?

HENRY: Well—originally—Originally I'm from Texas.

AMADO: Texas?

HENRY: Yes. "Home of the cowboys."

AMADO: Dallas, Texas?

HENRY: No. West. Van Horn. Way west.

AMADO: But when you go back, you will go back to Michigan?

HENRY: Yes.

AMADO: The home of your wife?

HENRY: That's right.

AMADO: So—*you* have no home, then?

HENRY: No—I mean—yes, of course I have a home!

AMADO: In Texas?

HENRY: No!

AMADO: Where, then?

HENRY: Stop asking me all these questions! It's none of your business!

AMADO: You are one of the homeless.

HENRY: No! Of course I'm not homeless! Do I look like a homeless person to you? The homeless don't travel to Mexico! They don't—go on vacation. Take planes and carry luggage around. They don't—Just—just leave me alone now! All right? It was very nice getting the opportunity to know someone like you—learning about your family—your history, your affairs of the heart and all that, but—I need to get out of here! Do you understand? *Comprende usted?* I need to *leave* this place. [*Pause. Amado lights a cigarette. Henry keeps packing.*]

AMADO: What if she has left Michigan—your wife. What if she has gone somewhere else?

HENRY: She won't leave Michigan. That's where she's from. That's where her mother's from. She'll never leave Michigan.

AMADO: What if her mother has died?

HENRY: Will you—[*Henry throws down a pair of socks and turns on Amado.*] Look—I have had about all I can stand from you. You hold me up in the middle of the night. You put a knife to my back. You take me prisoner. You threaten me with outrageous barbarism! And now, you stand here, in the middle of my room, uninvited, and harangue me with questions about my personal life! Who in the hell do you think you are!

AMADO: I am a simple man.

HENRY: No! No, not so simple. Devious and treacherous is more like it. What are you trying to do to me exactly? What is it you want from me?

AMADO: I am trying to save you, Mr. Henry. [*Pause.*]

HENRY: Save me? You're trying to save me? Save me from what? Who are *you* to be trying to save *me?* You're a bandit, for Christ's sake.

AMADO: You will not find her when you go back. She will not be there.

HENRY: What? My wife? You don't know that. How could you possibly know something like that?

AMADO: I can *see*. It is already too late. Much too late.

HENRY: Too late for what!

AMADO: Too late to retrieve what you have already lost.

HENRY: It's not too late! There's still a connection between us. Still some—thread.

AMADO: She is gone from there. She has left Michigan.

HENRY: What're you talking about! I just—spoke to her on the phone a week ago.

AMADO: Many things can happen in a week.

HENRY: Nothing's happened! We've just decided to be apart for a while. It was mutual. We both thought it was time—to think things over. There was nothing—final about it.

AMADO: Your wife is far away.

HENRY: Stop saying that! Stop it! Stop tormenting me! I can't stand it. I didn't ask for this! [*Henry breaks down. Pause, as he weeps deeply.*]

AMADO: [*Kindly.*] Now you are weeping, Mr. Henry.

HENRY: Yes—yes, I am.

AMADO: Why do you weep? You are on vacation. You should not weep.

HENRY: [*Between sobs.*] I—I just—I don't know what to do. I'm not feeling very stable right now. I—I keep having this terrible dream. It keeps waking me up. I can't stop seeing it. Over and over. For days now—I wake up in a cold sweat.

AMADO: What dream is that, Mr. Henry?

HENRY: [*Controlling himself.*] This nightmare. I've never had anything like this kind of dream before. It just started since I've been down here. I don't—It keeps repeating. I'm shaking from it now. Just thinking about it. It's somehow—connected—y'know, connected to my wife.

AMADO: What is it? What's in your dream?

HENRY: [*Pause, getting a hold of himself.*] The Devil. I see him. I know it's him. I don't even believe in the Devil or—God, or heaven or—any of that stuff. You know—I mean, I'm not a religious person. Never have been really. I mean, they dragged me to church when I was a kid—had no choice about that. They stuck me in the choir. Black robes and white collars. Had to get down on my knees and sing. Squeeze my hands together until they turned blue. You know, but—belief—faith—I had nothing like that. I—I had concepts about God, I guess. Infinity. The afterlife. All that stuff. I'd make up things in my head. But then, when I got older, of course—all that left me. I was off and running. I—

I—I had ambition. Ambition, I guess. That's what took over. That was "God" enough for me, I wanted—well you know— I wanted to make my mark. Accumulate some power. Prestige. Get a little nest egg. Start my own little dynasty. And all that—all that was going along just perfectly. Real estate. The market. The Dow. Just like I'd planned it. Better than I'd planned it, actually. It was snowballing beyond my wildest dreams. I couldn't get enough of it. And then—and then I met my wife. And that was the—ultimate, I guess. I never thought I'd meet someone like this. I mean, I'd dreamed about it. I had visions of meeting a woman like this but never thought I'd—And there she was. Suddenly, she came into my life. I couldn't believe—I couldn't believe it was actually happening. We had—I became overwhelmed. Obsessed. She had this quality about her. This—honesty. She actually knew who she was. She belonged to herself. That's what it was. She was her own person. And I—wanted that—that thing—whatever it was she had. I wanted to possess it. I wanted to take it away from her and make it my own. I wanted to actually rob her of herself. That's what I wanted to do. It became my new ambition.

AMADO: So you—*You* are a bandit, Mr. Henry?

HENRY: Yes. Yes I am. I was. I took her out into the country. Deep into the country so I didn't have to share her with anyone. Just the two of us. We bought a place out there. She had no friends. We lived completely isolated. I would screen all her calls. Sort through her mail. She was never out of my sight. And for a while—for a while it was exciting. It lasted—for a while, like that. But then—she began pulling away. She wanted to go off on trips by herself. I couldn't understand. She said she wanted to visit some friends in New York and I couldn't understand that. Why would she want to see anyone else? *I* didn't need to see anyone else. Why should she? I took it as a sign of deep betrayal. Abandonment. She was leaving. I called her a traitor. I turned her into my terrible enemy. *I* did that. It was *me*. I was the one who did that.

AMADO: You were losing your mind, Mr. Henry.

HENRY: Yes. Yes, that's what it was. I was actually losing my mind. I wanted to kill her. Can you imagine?

AMADO: So now the Devil, he comes to you?

HENRY: Yes. Every night. I see him. He comes and he—smiles at me. He's got this terrible sadness in his eyes. This heart-breaking sadness, as though he's a prisoner of something. As though he'll never be released. And I—feel sorry for him.

AMADO: Sorry?

HENRY: I do. Yes. In the dream. I have this feeling as though I'd like to—help him in some way. Ease his suffering. And as I begin to make a move toward him, he turns his back on me and looks back over his shoulder at me as though he wants me to follow him. Like he's going to lead me some-where. He's very short and stocky. Muscular almost. And his back—his back is covered with all these short brown squirming things—like hook worms or something. They're all over his back, living in his skin. Parasites, wriggling. And right at the base of his spine is one large one of these things, much bigger than the rest, growing right out of the base of his spine with a life of its own.

AMADO: That is his tail.

HENRY: Yes! That's exactly what it was. His tail. That's how I knew who he was. That's how I knew! You've seen him then too?

AMADO: Of course.

HENRY: He comes to you? Visits you like that? In a dream?

AMADO: He visits me, yes. Sometimes he travels with me.

HENRY: You know him well then?

AMADO: Yes.

HENRY: You speak to him?

AMADO: We have—an understanding.

HENRY: Why would he visit *me*? Why *me*? I haven't done any-thing—I'm a good person.

AMADO: Mr. Henry, you must pass beyond this sorrow. This dream is just part of the sign.

HENRY: What sign!

AMADO: That your wife is gone.

HENRY: What are you saying! What's happening to me! Why is this happening to me! [*Henry collapses with his back to Amado. Pause. Amado approaches him gently.*]

AMADO: Last night—down on the street—The moment you turned your face to me and showed me your eyes, I knew. I could see it.

HENRY: See what? What could you see? I can't see anything!

AMADO: You have been sent to me.

HENRY: No! NO, NO, NO, NO, NO!!! I refuse! I absolutely refuse to be a party to this! I have to get back to my wife! Don't you understand that? Don't you have the least bit of— compassion.

AMADO: I have compassion for the truth, Mr. Henry. You refuse to see the truth.

HENRY: How could this be? [*Pause.*] How could this possibly be?

AMADO: You have to turn yourself around. Can you do that? Can you turn yourself completely around and face me? [*Pause. Slowly Henry turns and faces Amado.*] Now—What do you see? Do you see a demon? Do you see an animal crea- ture? Do you see a despised soul, lower than a sick dog? Something to kick in the street? What do you see, Mr. Henry?

HENRY: I—I don't know you.

AMADO: No. Unknown. Completely unknown. And isn't it true you have no idea what's in store for you? No idea what- soever?

HENRY: I—have thoughts about the future.

AMADO: The future. Your wife and you.

HENRY: Yes. My family.

AMADO: Back together.

HENRY: Yes. Of course.

AMADO: Even though you've been separated all this time. Even though when you were together you were not happy.

HENRY: We were—happy. Once.

AMADO: Once. In a dream.

HENRY: In the past.

AMADO: In a dream of the past. And now this dream has filled you up. This dream based on some little fragment—some little moment when your lips might have touched hers and lightning crashed through your body. Long, long ago, Mr. Henry.

HENRY: It was more than that.

AMADO: You carry this dream wherever you go so that you no longer see what's right in front of you. And this dream, based on a lie, based on all the many lies; you actually believe this dream will somehow deliver you to the truth? I am sorry for you, Mr. Henry. I am sorry for your whole country.

HENRY: It's not like that. It couldn't be like that. I see my predicament—I understand that I'm—I'm not trying to deny my confusion. I'm just—

AMADO: Love needs a sacrifice, Mr. Henry. That is all. There is no other way. Without this sacrifice there is no love.

HENRY: [*Pause.*] I don't understand.

AMADO: No. No, you don't. But I am here to deliver it to you. I have been sent to you and you, to me.

HENRY: But I didn't come down here with the intention of giving up my eyes! That was not my reason. I came down here to get away.

AMADO: There are forces beyond your reason.

HENRY: What good is it going to do? What good could it possibly do for me to forfeit my eyes to you? Is it going to suddenly make everything all right between me and my—Is it going to cause some kind of revelation or salvation or—what? What exactly is it going to do? You tell me.

AMADO: [*Pause.*] It will make my Consuela smile. [*Pause. Suddenly Henry goes to his luggage and starts throwing his clothes into the bag. Amado just watches him and makes no move to stop him.*]

HENRY: [*As he throws his bag together.*] All right! All right. If you're going to do this, there's nothing I can do about it. You might as well do it now. Sneak up behind me. Cut my throat! Do whatever you want. Go ahead. But I'm not going down without a fight! That's for sure. I'm not some kind of sacrificial lamb that's going to passively lay his head on the stone. You might think—You might actually think that I'm physically inferior to you in some way. Age or something. Well I'll tell you what, mister—I've kept myself pretty fit for a man in his fifties. We Americans—I mean—our whole—You underestimate the tenacity; the sheer willpower; the toughness that we still possess. I mean—you might be right about certain other qualities; other weaknesses of character, but in that area of doggedness and determination and pure old-

fashioned grit, well you're up against a pretty tough cus-
tomer. We don't just roll over and play dead when the chips
are down. No siree. You don't see us sneaking off into other
people's countries; swimming rivers and what have you in
order to make a living. We fight! And that's the truth of it.
We fight for every inch of what we've established. And we'll
continue to fight right down to the wire. Come hell or high
water! So you just try and cut my eyeballs out, mister. You
just go ahead and try it. [*Consuela suddenly appears, riding a
bicycle onstage from downstage left. She stops directly in front of
the boardinghouse and just stands there, straddling the bike, and
stares into the room. Henry sees her and stops cold. He rushes to
the edge of the room and stares out at her. She stares back. Pause.
To Amado.*] Is that—That's not your woman is it? This—Consuela? Is that her? Answer me! [*Amado crosses slowly downstage beside Henry and stares out at her. He smiles.*] Is that her!
She's—She's only a child. [*Amado just smiles. Henry rushes to
his suitcase, picks it up and exits the room after Consuela. As he
goes, his small blue American passport falls to the floor. Amado
turns and sees it lying there. Henry rushes toward Consuela,
who is already riding the bike halfway up the road. Henry stops
her. To Consuela, carrying his suitcase.*] No, wait! Wait a second, please! Please—I just have to speak to you for a
moment. Un momento, por favor. Es muy importante. [*Consuela stops and waits for him to catch up. He keeps a hold of his
suitcase. Approaching Consuela.*] Por favor—es su nombre Consuela? Is that it? I'm sorry, I don't speak very well. I'm not—
fluent. I just uh—If you are who I think you are, it's very
important that I talk to you. [*Consuela just stares at him,
showing no sign of emotion. No smile. Pause. Viejo cracks the
door of the boardinghouse and peers out at Henry and Consuela.
Just his face is seen in eerie half-light. Henry doesn't notice him.
To Consuela.*] I've been—abducted somehow—or uh—kid-
napped—captured! That's it. I've been captured. "Captivo,"

entiende? That's what's happened to me. I'm a prisoner of some kind. Uh—it seems that your husband—your man is under the impression that I have something you need. Something you've asked him to collect for you, for some unfathomable reason. And I—I just want to clear this up once and for all. And—Is this making any kind of sense to you at all? Am I—getting through? Your *esposo*—[*Sees that he's getting nowhere.*] Oh, my God! My God, my God, my God! [*Consuela just stares at him, astride the bike. In the room Amado crosses to Henry's passport and picks it up. He leafs through the pages. Viejo keeps peeking out through the door. To Consuela.*] Look—Look—I want you to see something. I want you to take a look at something. Okay? [*Henry sets down the suitcase and places his fingers and thumbs around his eyes, stretching them wide open so Consuela can see their color. She starts to leave on the bike. Stretching his eyes open.*] No! No, don't be afraid. I'm trying to show you something, that's all. [*Consuela stops again and stares at Henry. Showing her his eyes.*] Take a look. Mira, por favor. Take a close look at my eyes. Can you see? The color? Don't be afraid. It's very important. You could correct this whole situation for me. Just tell him that he's on the wrong track. I don't know why he can't see it for himself but sometimes, I guess, a man just gets obsessed with an idea and won't let go of it. He just keeps chewing on it and chewing on it and chewing on it until it eats him up. You could reason with him. Tell him he's dead wrong. He'd listen to you. [*Consuela just stares at him. Henry drops his hands from his eyes. Amado crosses to hammock in the room and lies on it, leafing through Henry's passport. To Consuela.*] I'm at the—end of my rope here. I don't know what to do. [*Pause, Henry exhausted, looks around, Viejo still peering out, unnoticed by Henry.*] Let me just ask you something. Just out of curiosity—How in the world—How could you have asked him to do such a thing? You're so—young. So—beautiful. Where did this idea of yours—this—this—whim—come from, anyway? You just woke up one morning with this thing in your head? This— horrible thing? [*Consuela starts to ride away again. Henry stops her, grabbing the handlebars.*] No! Don't leave! Please, don't leave. [*Pause.*] Could I—Do you think it might be possible for me to borrow your bicycle? Just to—Just for a short while. I'll see that it's returned to you. I promise. [*Pause. She just stares at him.*]

CONSUELA: Where will you go? [*Henry is somewhat shocked by hearing Consuela talk. He lets go of the bike and straightens up.*]

HENRY: Where? I—isn't there a road or something that leads out of here? I mean, a taxi brought me in here. There must be a road!

CONSUELA: You are standing on it.

HENRY: [*Looks down at his feet.*] Yes. So I am? This is it? All I have to do is—follow this out of here? Just—

CONSUELA: It's not so easy. [*Consuela takes off fast on the bike and disappears before Henry can do anything about it. He chases her a few steps, then stops and turns back toward his suitcase.*]

HENRY: [*Chasing.*] No, wait! Wait! Please! [*He stands there a while, then crosses to his suitcase, picks it up. He turns in a circle, lost. Pause. Viejo comes out onto the porch. Henry sees him.*]

VIEJO: Are you—taking another one of your walks, my friend?

HENRY: No. I—I was trying to find a way out of here.

VIEJO: Were you talking to your wife again? I heard you speaking to someone.

HENRY: No. No, I wasn't. I was speaking to a girl.

VIEJO: A girl?

HENRY: Yes. That girl—Consuela. She was here.

VIEJO: Consuela?

HENRY: That's right. She was just here on her bicycle.

VIEJO: [*Laughs.*] She has been visiting again!

HENRY: Visiting? Look—I need to pay for my room now. I need to settle up and get out of here.

VIEJO: You are leaving us so soon?

HENRY: It's not so soon! It's not soon enough as far as I'm concerned. I need to pay up and get out. I need to call a cab. A taxi. Do you think you could do that for me? Call a taxi?

VIEJO: There is no phone, señor.

HENRY: Oh, come on, there must be a phone. There's got to be a phone somewhere in this village. What do people do here in a state of emergency?

VIEJO: There are no emergencies here, my friend.

HENRY: What are you talking about? What about birth! What about death! What about rattlesnakes and scorpions! Broken bones! There's emergencies all over the place. This whole country is one big fat festering emergency! And even if there are no emergencies, through some weird miracle or another, I myself happen to be in the middle of a very dire emergency right now. Right this very second. Can you understand that?

VIEJO: You are not bleeding, my friend.

HENRY: No. No, that's true. I am *not* bleeding. That's very true. There are—There do happen to be other categories of emergency beyond the flesh and blood. There's emergencies of the—Never mind! Can you help me or not!

VIEJO: She was riding a bicycle?

HENRY: Yes. Yes, she was. And—I don't know—she caught me by surprise. I wasn't expecting to meet her.

VIEJO: Are you sure it was her? Consuela?

HENRY: It had to be her. She was—just like he described her.

VIEJO: Did she speak to you, my friend?

HENRY: Yes—Yes, she did.

VIEJO: You are lucky, my friend.

HENRY: Lucky? *I'm* lucky?

VIEJO: Very rarely does a *Sombra* speak.

HENRY: [*Pause.*] *"Sombra"*?

VIEJO: *Un Fantasma.* Consuela was my daughter. She was shot through the heart by the man who swings in your hammock. That same bullet passed through my eye and left me with half a world. [*Pause. Amado gets out of the hammock and just stands there, looking out, still holding Henry's passport.*] Now he is a man caught between two stools. He can never rest.

HENRY: [*Pause.*] No—Look—I—I am an ordinary man. Just a plain old everyday average ordinary American man. I come from an ordinary background. Generations of ordinariness. There is nothing—absolutely nothing inside me that can even begin to comprehend this stuff. I don't want to be involved in this type of thing. I simply want to return to the *known world*. Something safe and simple. My wife. My children. My house. My car. My dog. The front lawn. My mobile phone! The Internet! Things I can put my fingers on. Tangible things in the real world! [*Amado begins to move slowly out of the room and into the street, carrying Henry's passport. Henry doesn't notice him. To Viejo.*] Do you understand me? I don't want to be dealing with madness now. Ghosts and sacrifices! Superstition and visions. We're approaching the millennium here! Things have moved beyond all that. Don't you have any concept at all of the outside world? The global perspective? The Bigger Picture! The *todo el mundo!* There's been an explosion of information out there! It's available to anybody now. Even people in the jungle. People like you. People completely removed from civilization. There's no secrets. There's no hocus-pocus. Everybody knows everything there is to know about absolutely everything! Electricity has delivered us! We're on the verge of breaking into territories never dreamed of before. Territories beyond the imagination. Things which will set us free so we don't have to be gouging each other's eyes out. So we don't have to be torturing and butchering each other like a bunch of diseased animals. So we don't have to be lost out

here—totally lost and—wandering—without—without a clue—
where we stand—in the scheme of things. Just completely—
cut off. [*Pause. Amado has arrived near Viejo and Henry, who
is beginning to pant with exhaustion and stress. Amado taps the
passport gently on his leg.*]

AMADO: Mr. Henry? [*Henry doesn't turn but looks up as though
hearing a disembodied voice.*] Mr. Henry, have you forgotten
something? [*Henry slowly turns to Amado, in a daze.*]

HENRY: [*Pause.*] Forgotten? No what have I forgotten? I've forgotten everything. I'm trying to settle my bill here.

AMADO: [*Holding up passport.*] Your—passport?

HENRY: [*Stares at passport.*] Oh—Is that mine? How'd that happen? I must've dropped it.

AMADO: You *did* drop it.

HENRY: Oh—Well, lotta good it's going to do me now. I'm not
going anywhere, am I? Thank you. [*Henry crosses to Amado,
takes hold of passport, but Amado won't let go of it.*]

AMADO: I was looking at your photograph. Your snapshot.
[*Henry tugs on passport, but Amado won't let go.*]

HENRY: Yes? What about it?

AMADO: Have you seen it lately?

HENRY: My picture? No. Why should I? It's the same picture
I've had for years. Look, could I please have my passport
back? [*Amado releases it. Henry takes it.*] Thank you very much.

AMADO: You should look at your photograph again, Mr. Henry. It might remind you.

HENRY: Remind me of what?

AMADO: Take a look. [*Henry turns page in passport and stares at his picture.*]

HENRY: What about it? It's me—It's always been me. Younger. I had a smile then. I actually—had a smile. I was in love.

AMADO: Your eyes, Mr. Henry—What color are your eyes in the photograph? [*Pause. Henry stares at passport. Viejo lights a cigarette.*]

HENRY: They're—They're—

AMADO: Blue. Yes?

HENRY: [*Staring at photo.*] They—seem to be. Yes. I think they are.

VIEJO: [*Snatching passport away from Henry.*] Let me see.

HENRY: Give me that! [*Viejo turns his back on Henry and keeps passport. He stares at photo.*]

AMADO: Blue eyes. How could that be?

VIEJO: Blue. *Sí. Es verdad.* Blue as the pale sky. [*Viejo hands passport back to Henry. Henry takes it and looks again.*]

HENRY: I don't know. I—maybe—

AMADO: Maybe what?

HENRY: The light or something. Age. It could be any number of things.

VIEJO: [*To Amado.*] Age and the light. It's possible.

HENRY: Everything changes—I mean—This was taken some time ago. The film might have faded.

AMADO: Blue eyes and an American passport. There was a time when I might have killed for these two things.

VIEJO: Very hard to come by, these two. You must be born into this privilege.

HENRY: Look, I would gladly trade all of it everything—if— [*Pause.*]

AMADO: If what, Mr. Henry?

HENRY: [*Pause.*] If I knew—If I could get some guarantee—

AMADO: Guarantee?

HENRY: Yes. That I could get out of here. That I could get safely back. Return—

AMADO: You would trade?

HENRY: I don't know—I don't know why I said that.

AMADO: But you *did* say that.

VIEJO: He did say that. I heard him say that.

HENRY: It was just—an impulse. That's all. I suddenly felt as though I would give anything—absolutely anything to get out of here. Even my—Where is she? Where is she right now?

AMADO: Oh, she's around.

VIEJO: She's always around.

HENRY: And you can call her back here?

AMADO: Yes, of course.

HENRY: All right. All right. If that's the case then—let's call her back. [*Amado turns abruptly upstage and whistles loudly. Pause. Consuela walks the bicycle onstage from upstage left and stops center stage. She stares at them without expression, holding the bike by the handlebars. Pause. Guitar comes into background softly.*]

AMADO: [*To Henry.*] What is it you would like to ask her, Mr. Henry?

HENRY: Well—well first of all, is it—is it at all possible that she might be able to lead me out of here. Ask her that. [*Amado turns toward Consuela and speaks to her in Spanish. Consuela makes absolutely no change in her expressionless face. Not the slightest hint of emotion as she listens.*]

AMADO: [*To Consuela, in Spanish.*] This man with the blue eyes would like to know from the depths of his heart whether you could lead him out of his misery. [*No response from Consuela. She just stands there holding the bike. Guitar continues underneath. Amado turns to Henry. To Henry, in English.*] She is not sure.

HENRY: Let her speak for herself. She can speak! I heard her.

VIEJO: She is very shy.

HENRY: [*To Amado.*] Ask her—Ask her if she knows anything at all about my—family. About my wife.

AMADO: [*To Consuela, in Spanish.*] This man with the blue eyes would like to know if you have any news of his family. [*No response from Consuela. Amado turns back to Henry. To Henry, in English.*] She has no news.

HENRY: Why doesn't she speak! Why doesn't she at least show some sign! Some human—sign!

VIEJO: She has grown very tired of human beings.

HENRY: [*To Viejo.*] *You* ask her, then. You're her father. Ask her if we can work some sort of trade. [*Amado pulls out his knife and a whetstone and begins sharpening it in small circular motions, spitting on the stone and rubbing the blade.*]

VIEJO: I cannot speak to her. I don't know the language.

HENRY: Speak Spanish! Speak English. I don't care. Anything!

VIEJO: It is not so simple.

HENRY: I'll ask her, then. [*Moving toward Consuela.*] Look— Consuela! Listen to me. [*Henry stops and speaks to her. Consuela just stands there with bike, staring at him. Guitar continues. Amado keeps sharpening knife. Viejo slips up behind Henry very quietly. Continuing to Consuela.*] I don't know what this strange desire of yours is but—say for instance, just for the sake of— what if I were to suddenly agree? What if I were to say, "Okay—all right—let's go ahead with this." I'll just let this man gouge my eyes out and hand them over to you. What if I were to say that? Would you then agree to get me the hell out of here? Would you show me the way to the airport or the taxi or some—some means of escape? [*Pause. No response from Consuela. She just stares at him. Guitar continues. Amado keeps up the rhythmic sharpening of the knife. Turning away from Consuela.*] No. No, see she—She has no intention of making any kind of deal with me! [*Viejo suddenly grabs Henry's arms from behind and holds him with a strength beyond his years. Amado keeps sharpening the knife and moves toward Henry. To Viejo.*] What're you doing! What's going on here!

AMADO: She is no fool, Mr. Henry.

HENRY: [*Struggling but not breaking loose.*] What is this!

AMADO: Did you think your false voice would convince her? Your squirming fear?

HENRY: [*Struggling.*] Let go of me!

AMADO: She has heard many men crying out in the night. Just like you. Many men falling to their knees. Kissing the dirt at her feet. Forsaking their children. Their wives. Their mothers. Even their Gods. She has watched them crawl for miles; blood squirting from their skulls. Moaning like cattle under the moon. She has never made a "deal" with any of them. Why should she begin with you?

HENRY: [*Being held by Viejo.*] Because—Because—I—Because I'm in sympathy with her! I know what her sorrow is all about! I know why she needs this—this—[*Pause.*]

AMADO: [*Closing in on him.*] Then you will be able to give it to her with the generosity of your whole heart. [*Viejo grabs Henry's hair from behind and jerks his head back in preparation for Amado, who continues sharpening the knife. Consuela stays and continues to watch impassively. Guitar continues.*]

HENRY: [*In Viejo's clutches.*] I AM NOT A VICTIM!!

AMADO: [*Closer to Henry with the knife.*] You will be able to step across the border. Into the light.

HENRY: I WILL BE BLIND FOREVER!! [*Through this, Amado is right on top of Henry, who remains held fast by Viejo. Amado slowly weaves the knife back and forth very close over Henry's eyes, like a hypnotist. Henry follows the blade. Guitar builds underneath. Consuela stays with bike, watching.*]

AMADO: You are blind now. Now! In *this* world. You do not see. [*Suddenly Consuela drops the bicycle. It crashes to the ground. The guitar stops. Silence. Viejo releases Henry. Amado drops his arms and backs away from Henry. They all stare at Consuela. Pause. Consuela moves very quickly downstage and goes right up to Henry. The others back away. Consuela takes Henry's face and holds it between her hands. She stares into his eyes. She moves her thumbs slowly under Henry's eyes, peering into them. She backs away from him.*]

CONSUELA: They are not blue. They have never been blue. [*Pause.*] They never will be. [*Consuela moves back upstage to the bike. She turns back and looks at all of them for a moment, then bends down, picks up the bicycle and walks it offstage. Pause. The others just stand there, staring after her.*]

VIEJO: She has always been a very generous girl. [*Viejo crosses to his rocking chair and sits. He lights a cigarette and <u>begins to rock slowly</u>. Pause.*]

AMADO: [*To Henry.*] I must have been mistaken.

HENRY: These things happen.

AMADO: I was so sure—Your passport. All the signs were there.

HENRY: Yes. I started to believe it myself.

AMADO: It's been so long since I've been able to make her smile.

HENRY: Well—maybe—There'll always be another tourist.

AMADO: Mr. Henry—

HENRY: Yes?

AMADO: I have a feeling I was wrong about your wife too. I have a feeling she is waiting for you. [*Amado goes to Henry's suitcase and picks it up. He crosses to Henry carrying the suitcase and stops in front of him.*] I will take you to a taxi.

HENRY: No—No, that's all right. I'll—I'll manage.

AMADO: Please. It would be my pleasure. [*Amado, carrying Henry's suitcase starts to lead him offstage right. Henry follows. Viejo stops them.*]

VIEJO: [*In rocker.*] Where are you going now, my friend?

HENRY: I'm—I'm going back to Michigan.

VIEJO: [*Rocking slowly.*] But you have not paid me your rent. Did you think this was a free vacation?

HENRY: [*Fishing for his wallet.*] Oh, I'm—I'm sorry. Of course. I'd completely forgotten. How much—How much did it come to? [*Henry moves toward Viejo with his wallet out. Amado stays behind with the suitcase.*]

VIEJO: [*Laughing.*] I don't want your money. Your money is no good in this place. [*Henry stops, still with his wallet out. Pause. He looks back at Amado then back to Viejo.*]

HENRY: [*To Viejo.*] What, then? How can I pay you?

VIEJO: [*Rocking.*] Your things! [*Pointing to suitcase.*] Your valuable things.

HENRY: [*Turning back to Amado.*] Oh—well—

VIEJO: I thought you said you had many valuable things.

HENRY: I do. Yes. Yes, of course.

VIEJO: Family heirlooms. Things you have carried your whole life.

HENRY: Yes.

VIEJO: Things you were willing to trade for your life. Back when you thought you were about to lose it.

HENRY: Yes—That's—true—

VIEJO: Then give them to me now. It's a very small price to pay, no?

HENRY: [*Pause.*] All right—That's fine—I'll go along with that. [*Henry crosses to Amado and takes the suitcase from him. He crosses back up to Viejo and sets the suitcase down beside him. Viejo smiles.*]

VIEJO: Thank you, my friend. Now you can return to Michigan with nothing.

HENRY: Yes. [*Henry crosses back down to Amado. They are about to exit when Viejo stops them again.*]

VIEJO: Mr. Henry. [*Henry turns to him. Pause.*] When you return to Michigan, you will see the snow with new eyes. Buena suerte, amigo. [*Henry and Amado exit. Guitar comes in again as lights begin to dim. Viejo bends down and opens Henry's suitcase. He pulls out some clothing and tosses it on the ground as he searches through the contents. He begins to pull out a sky-blue silken scarf that never ends, like the old circus scarves that clowns used. He keeps pulling it out onto the floor, but it won't stop coming. Slowly Consuela emerges on foot from upstage left and crosses to the scarf. She bends down, picks up the free end and carries it offstage. The scarf keeps moving, flowing from the suitcase offstage in a constant river of blue motion. Lights keep dimming to black. Viejo keeps rocking. Guitar underneath.*]

When the World Was Green

(A Chef's Fable)

BY JOSEPH CHAIKIN AND SAM SHEPARD

"We began as a mineral. We emerged into plant life, and into the animal state, and then into being human, and always we have forgotten our former states, except in early spring when we slightly recall being green again."

—*Rumi (A.D. 1207–1273)*

When the World Was Green was originally commissioned and produced by the Atlanta Committee for the Olympic Games Cultural Olympiad for the Olympic Arts Festival in conjunction with 7 Stages, Atlanta, in 1996. It was produced in New York by Signature Theatre Company (James Houghton, Founding Artistic Director; Thomas C. Proehl, Managing Director; Elliot Fox, Associate Director) on October 22, 1996, with the following cast:

OLD MAN	Alvin Epstein
INTERVIEWER	Amie Quigley
PIANIST	Woody Regan

Directed by Joseph Chaikin
Designed by Christine Jones
Costumes by Mary Brecht
Lighting by Beverly Emmons
Music composed by Woody Regan

Characters:

INTERVIEWER—Young woman, about 25, wears dress of neutral color.

OLD MAN—In his sixties or seventies, wears a muted blue prisoner's uniform, no stripes.

Time: The recent past.

Place: A prison cell in an unnamed country.

The cell is represented by a broad, murky gray wall which covers the entire upstage rear. The wall is broken only by a tall, slit-like window in its center which allows in minimal light. There is no indication of a door for entry or of prison bars. Furniture in the cell consists only of a simple wooden chair set in front of a small square wood table upstage left, and the Old Man's cell bed, positioned down right at an angle to the back wall. On the bed is a thin mattress, no sheets or pillow.

NOTES ON PERFORMING

The Action: We never see the characters enter or leave the cell.

The Solos: Solos by the Interviewer and the Old Man occur between some of the Visits and are lit as indicated. The Old Man's Solos take place within the cell. The Interviewer's Solos are played along the sides of the stage, "outside" the cell.

The Storytelling: When the Old Man tells his stories to the Interviewer, he sometimes faces toward the audience but he always remains in character.

The Music: For the premiere, a *minimal* live piano score was devised to highlight the intense moments of storytelling and to allude indirectly to the Old Man's cousin who played the piano.

First Visit

INTERVIEWER: How did this all begin?

OLD MAN: There was an insult.

INT.: When?

O.M.: Many years ago. Two hundred years ago, I think.

INT.: That long?

O.M.: Yes.

INT.: Where did this insult take place?

O.M.: In an open field. So they told me.

INT.: And it was your great-great-great-grandfather? Is that right?

O.M.: Maybe. Nobody's sure now.

INT.: How many generations?

O.M.: Many.

INT.: You don't remember?

O.M.: I wasn't there. I wasn't born.

INT.: But somebody told you, from your family?

O.M.: Yes.

INT.: It was handed down?

O.M.: Yes. My father told me.

INT.: And his father told him?

O.M.: Yes. In our country, it takes seven generations or one hundred years for an insult to come to an end. Whichever comes first. And then only a woman can end it.

INT.: A woman?

O.M.: Yes. All a woman has to do is remove the scarf from her head and wave it in the air and all bloodshed must stop.

INT.: Why a woman?

O.M.: She has the power to give birth, so only she can stop death.

INT.: And what was this original insult?

O.M.: Many, many years ago when the world was green, my great-great-great-great-grandfather was working in an open field with his mule. And this mule had caused some trouble in the village but he was a good worker, an honest worker, so my great-great-great-grandfather kept him and forgave him his trespasses.

INT.: This was your great-great-great-great-grandfather? How many "greats"?

O.M.: Nobody's sure anymore. It's been so long.

INT.: And what was the trouble with this mule?

O.M.: He'd been breaking out of his pen and eating the neighbor's crops.

INT.: I see. So your great-great-great-great-grandfather couldn't keep him in?

O.M.: No. And one day—this one particular day, the birds were singing, the sun was out, there wasn't a cloud in the sky— the mule fell over dead in front of my grandfather's plow. He just dropped dead.

INT.: Heart attack?

O.M.: Poison.

INT.: Poison?

O.M.: Yes. His tongue was swollen the size of a loaf of bread.

INT.: Who poisoned him?

O.M.: The neighbor. A family. They were related to us, but they became our enemy on that day. They have always been our enemy. All this time.

INT.: Generations.

O.M.: Yes. Forever.

INT.: And the man you killed—the mistaken man—you thought he was part of this family.

O.M.: I was sure of it. I'd been tracking him all my life.

INT.: But the man you murdered was the wrong man.

O.M.: That's what they say, yes.

INT.: How could that happen?

O.M.: I've asked myself the same question. He was always disguising himself, changing his identity, in order to trick me. Apparently he did.

INT.: And you poisoned the man? The wrong man?

O.M.: Yes.

INT.: You concocted the poison yourself? That's what they said in the paper.

O.M.: Yes. I am a cook. A chef. I know about these things.

INT.: So you put the poison in his food.

O.M.: Yes. Potatoes. Potatoes are easiest.

INT.: But you killed the wrong man.

O.M.: That's what they tell me. It makes no difference now.

INT.: What do you mean?

O.M.: It's done. It's finished. I've exhausted myself.

INT.: Don't you feel some regret? Remorse? Particularly since the man was completely innocent.

O.M.: No. Just exhaustion.

INT.: Did you talk with the victim's family?

O.M.: No. I don't want to see anyone. I didn't want to see you. How did you get in? Who are you, exactly?

INT.: I'm writing a story on you.

O.M.: What story?

INT.: The story of how you came to do this thing.

O.M.: It's not interesting.

INT.: To me it is.

O.M.: Why? Why would you be interested in me?

INT.: You remind me of myself.

O.M.: How? You're young. Just beginning.

INT.: I've also been on a search for a long time.

O.M.: What sort of search?

INT.: My father disappeared when I was very young.

O.M.: Oh, I see. And you've been hunting for him?

INT.: Yes. I've followed endless clues. That's why I was drawn to your case. You tracked this man your whole life.

O.M.: Yes. But it's not the same. I was born into it. Destined.

INT.: When did you first learn that you were supposed to kill him?

o.m.: When I was five years old. My father told me I had to kill him.

int.: Did he describe the victim to you?

o.m.: Yes. He was my cousin, so I already knew him. We grew up together. We were in the same school.

int.: You were cousins?

o.m.: Yes. Related by blood through my mother.

int.: You were the same age?

o.m.: Yes.

int.: And did this boy know that you intended to kill him? Back when you were children together.

o.m.: Oh, yes. Our families both knew. It was a game we played. Disguises. Hiding. We made jokes about it. It all started back then.

int.: Did you try to kill him when you were a child?

o.m.: No. I waited.

int.: You were afraid?

o.m.: No. I wanted to be stronger. Bigger and stronger.

int.: But you waited so long.

o.m.: He kept eluding me. He got to be very clever.

INT.: Did you enjoy hunting him?

O.M.: It was my whole life. Now it's finished.

End First Visit

OLD MAN SOLO

O.M.: [*To audience.*] She thinks there's some secret I'm keeping,
but I have no secret. If you ask me where I've been, I can
only say seasons and shapes of trees—windows I've watched
from. Pigeons. Time all rolls together. I've lost all touch
with my people. The village I left has changed governments
ten times. Each new government claims new corpses. My
family has all been lost. Why does she care? If you ask me to
trace my steps—to follow myself through countries and
trains and stations—all I have is the sensation of growing
fatigue. I've come to the end of myself and I can't sleep. I'm
exhausted and wide awake.

Second Visit

INT.: I've brought you some doughnuts.

O.M.: No thanks.

INT.: You should eat. They tell me you're not eating anything.

O.M.: Food doesn't interest me anymore.

INT.: Aren't you hungry?

O.M.: My stomach growls, but I don't feel hunger. Why have you come back?

INT.: To continue.

O.M.: Don't you have better things to do? You're young. Don't you have boyfriends? Movies? Dancing?

INT.: I want to write this story.

O.M.: There is no story.

INT.: We'll find it as we go along.

O.M.: There's nothing to invent. It's very simple. I killed the wrong man. Now it's over.

INT.: Aren't you interested in who this man was?

O.M.: His life has no more meaning than my own. And you? You love your work? All these questions.

INT.: Yes. It fascinates me. Inquiring into people's lives.

O.M.: What do you hope to find?

INT.: Where are you from?

O.M.: The name?

INT.: Yes. What's it called?

o.m.: I'm from the village of Ameda in the mountain region. The weather there is perfect. The soil is perfect. The best fruits and nuts are raised there. The family is King.

int.: Is it mainly agricultural then?

o.m.: Yes. Farmers. Mostly farmers.

int.: So your family was working the land?

o.m.: Yes. But all I wanted to do was learn how to cook. From the time I was very little. I had a passion for it. My mother used to take me through the market every afternoon. She would pull me by the hand. I was very small. The wagons of vegetables and fruits hovered all around us like a forest. Fish, piled as high as a mountain, glistening in the sun. Game hanging from hooks. Heads of deer and pigs. And all around this world, this market, hovered the aromas of cooking. People cooking.

int.: What fascinated you about cooking?

o.m.: The transformation. Changing all these gifts from the earth into food.

int.: Do you have a specialty?

o.m.: Yes. Poultry. Duck, pheasant, goose. Things like that. Quail with Pear Amaretto sauce. That's one of my best.

int.: This cousin of yours—

o.m.: Carl.

INT.: Is that his name? The cousin you were intending to kill?

O.M.: Carl Loom.

INT.: What does he do?

O.M.: He's a musician. A piano player. He plays all over the world.

INT.: Concerts?

O.M.: Everywhere. Motels sometimes. Lobbies.

INT.: Motels?

O.M.: Yes. There was one motel where he was playing and I was cooking at the same time. That was funny.

INT.: You were both working in the same place?

O.M.: Yes. We used to laugh about it and make faces at each other. No one knew that we were related.

INT.: Did you try to kill him then?

O.M.: No. I was still planning it. Watching him eat. I wanted to make sure to choose the right kind of food.

INT.: You mean for the poison?

O.M.: Yes. He always finished his potatoes. He might leave some bread or meat or broccoli, but he always finished his potatoes.

INT.: Why did you decide to poison him rather than some other way?

o.m.: Like what?

int.: Shooting or stabbing, for instance.

o.m.: I've already told you. Because of the mule. They poisoned our mule. That was the beginning. Now all I want is to rest in peace. But I can't even sleep.

int.: Why aren't you sleeping?

o.m.: I don't know. Pictures.

int.: In your mind?

o.m.: Yes.

int.: Pictures of the victim?

o.m.: No. Birds. Faces. Crowds of people fleeing. Wind. The open sea. Things like that.

End Second Visit

OLD MAN SOLO

[*Old Man seated in the chair, facing audience, only upper body is lit.*]

o.m.: [*To audience.*] I was a boy, so they told me. They told me this because I refused to remember. They told me I was standing beside a well with some soldiers who were passing through our village. I don't know where these soldiers came from, but they were searching for something. They had been searching every well in the town, drawing up the buckets and poking their rifles into the fresh water. They told me I followed these soldiers from well to well until, finally, they found what they were looking for. This last bucket they pulled up contained what looked like raw meat floating in dark blood. They told me the soldiers laughed and fired their rifles into the clear sky when they discovered this bucket. They said it contained the testicles of their enemy. This is what they told me. I refuse to remember. To this day, I still refuse.

[*Fade to black.*]

Third Visit

[*Interviewer is unfolding a sheet and placing it on the bed, tucking it in, while Old Man sits on chair.*]

O.M.: What have you brought now?

INT.: Things to help you sleep. Pillows. Clean sheets.

O.M.: You don't have to do that. Why are you doing this?

INT.: It's no trouble. [*She starts making his bed.*]

O.M.: I don't understand this concern you have for me. You're from the paper.

INT.: I just thought that if you had fresh sheets and pillows you might be able to get some sleep.

O.M.: It won't help.

INT.: It's worth a try.

O.M.: [*Rises and moves downstage.*] It won't stop the thoughts.

INT.: [*Picks up colorful folded blanket and moves toward him.*] What are you thinking? What keeps you awake?

O.M.: Last night I dreamt of plants. Herbs. Especially sage. I could smell it in my dream. I could see it waving in the wind.

INT.: Sage?

O.M.: Magnificent.

INT.: [*Placing blanket on bed.*] I would like to help you get some sleep.

O.M.: I just want to be left alone.

INT.: I'm sorry. I thought I could help.

O.M.: You can't help.

INT.: But you need to eat and sleep. I brought you some fruit.

O.M.: Would you be doing this if I hadn't committed murder? If you just saw me wandering through a park or huddled on a bench? If you saw me rushing across a street to avoid an oncoming car?

INT.: No. I suppose not.

O.M.: So, you have a morbid curiosity about me, then?

INT.: No, I wouldn't say that.

O.M.: How old are you?

INT.: Twenty-five.

O.M.: Twenty-five.

INT.: Yes.

O.M.: I can't remember being twenty-five.

INT.: Where were you when you were my age?

O.M.: I must have been traveling. There was a period where I never stopped moving.

INT.: Trains?

O.M.: Yes.

INT.: You always took trains?

O.M.: When I could, yes. I liked the rhythm. The constant rhythm. The clackidy-clack.

INT.: You were following the trail of your cousin?

O.M.: Sometimes. Sometimes I would just ride. I would lose track and just ride to the end of the line and then get on another train.

INT.: You had no idea where it was going? The destination?

o.m.: Sometimes not. I was one of the lucky ones. I always managed to have a ticket. There were thousands without tickets. Running along beside the train. Terror in their eyes. Terror of being left behind.

int.: What would you do when you got to your destination?

o.m.: I would love to sample the food. Going from place to place. So many different tastes. In Egypt I sampled Samak Kamounieh—baked fish with cumin. Unforgettable. Corn breads in Kenya. Ethiopian Ataklete Kilkil—a very distinctive potato with nutmeg and turmeric. Peanut stew. Korean cabbage—Kimchi. So many, many worlds of flavor and texture.

int.: What was your favorite?

o.m.: Desserts. I would sit in cafés for hours testing desserts. Sometimes only one spoonful. Then another. Crème Brûlée. Raspberry Sorbet. Mocha Almond Fudge Cake.

int.: This must have been very expensive.

o.m.: Yes. When I ran out of money, I would get a job.

int.: Cooking?

o.m.: Yes. Or washing dishes sometimes. Just to be in the kitchen. Any job in the kitchen.

int.: So you were eating well back then, I guess.

o.m.: I never had any trouble eating when I was young.

int.: So, what happened? Why can't you eat now?

o.m.: I told you. It doesn't interest me. You have to be interested. The taste. The smell. Something. Now, when I look at an orange, I can't imagine the taste. I have no longing for it to be in my mouth. No desire. Like sex.

int.: Sex?

o.m.: I have no longing. No longing at all.

int.: What about sleep, though? You must long for sleep?

o.m.: Yes. But I can't remember what it's like.

int.: Do thoughts about the victim keep you awake?

o.m.: Sometimes. Sometimes I see him. Sitting there. Content. Breaking his bread. Staring out the café window. Stirring his coffee in a dream. I can't tell what he's thinking, but it's not troubled. It's a calm face. No worries. His newspaper is folded beside him. His glasses rest on the tablecloth. Everything is peaceful around him. Ordered. He sips his soup in the European way—tipping the bowl and spooning away from himself. He wipes his upper lip with the napkin and then brushes the crumbs off his chin very gently. He returns the napkin to the same knee and spreads it smoothly. I see his ring on his little finger flashing. A blue ring that sparkles from the sunlight through the window. A bird flits by outside, and his eyes rise to follow it, then return to the empty soup bowl. He pushes the bowl to one side with both hands, then reaches for the glass of water. He drinks and doesn't stop drinking until the glass is empty. I can see his throat throbbing as the icy water rushes through. His eyes close as though he's in an ecstasy and dreaming of something far away.

End Third Visit

INTERVIEWER SOLO

INT.: [*To audience.*] I was born by the river. Close to the river. Even as a baby, I could feel the pull of the green water. Always moving. I was raised by only women. Surrounded by women. No men. My mother, my aunt, my cousin, two sisters and my grandmother. We lived in the same house. No one ever spoke of men. No one ever asked about my father. His absence. The first man I ever saw was a fisherman who floated by in his boat. He waved to me. I waved back. He returned the next day and anchored his boat by the shore. I went down and asked him if he'd ever seen my father, and he told me he'd heard stories about him. There were many stories on the river. He told me that my father had got a job on a coal barge and gone down to New Orleans, but no one had ever heard from him since. I asked him how long the river was, and he said it went for miles. Clear down to the Gulf of Mexico. I asked him if he'd take me down there, but he only laughed and wiped the sweat from his hatband. I noticed how different his hands were from the hands of women.

Fourth Visit

INT.: You're still not eating?

O.M.: What do you enjoy? Fish? Poultry? Game?

INT.: No. No meat.

O.M.: A vegetarian.

INT.: Yes.

O.M.: Hitler was a vegetarian.

INT.: I didn't know that.

O.M.: It's hard for me to imagine being a vegetarian.

INT.: Why? There are so many foods on this earth. Nuts, fruits, grains. Why kill animals?

O.M.: It's part of a process. Hunting and cooking are all connected. They always have been.

INT.: Yes, but there are so many different foods.

O.M.: What do you enjoy especially?

INT.: Mangoes.

O.M.: Mango?

INT.: Yes. I adore mango. It's like food from heaven, don't you think?

O.M.: Well, I wouldn't go that far.

INT.: Golden. Soft. Sweet. It's almost impossible that it even exists. It's wonderful. Just the smell of it.

O.M.: Mango.

INT.: Yes. And another thing I love is mushrooms. Just appear after a good hard rain. So many kinds. Thousands, they say.

o.m.: Thousands? Yes, there must be.

int.: That's what they say. Thousands of different varieties.

o.m.: Yes. It's amazing. Like the stars.

int.: The colors and shapes. It's almost unimaginable.

o.m.: In Ameda we used to say God was throwing the stars. Organizing. He became inspired. Planets. Galaxies. Nebulae. Extraordinary variety. He was having fun. Ecstatic.

int.: God?

o.m.: Yes! So many varieties. Throwing them, like the stars. Species. Animals. Plants. Humans. Birds. Fish.

int.: Mushrooms?

o.m.: Yes! Mushrooms, too. And then, they say, God became exhausted. He had a permanent breakdown. And all variety ended. Things were fixed in their forms and shapes.

int.: Even mushrooms.

o.m.: Yes. Even mushrooms.

int.: I can almost smell them.

o.m.: They're good in sauce. Some sauces are entirely dependent on mushrooms.

int.: Yes, but I love them raw too. The different textures. Crisp sometimes. Very subtle.

o.m.: You're making me want to cook.

int.: Yes! Maybe we could have a meal together. Just the two of us.

o.m.: No, but I would like to cook something for you. I know a chutney with mango and almonds that's absolutely out of this world.

int.: I could bring you the ingredients. Just make a list.

o.m.: They won't allow it in here.

int.: Oh, I'm sure they would, under the circumstances. I'll talk to someone. I'll get permission.

o.m.: No. I'm very grateful to talk to you, but cooking is out of the question for me now.

int.: You must try to eat something.

o.m.: Isn't it funny, the imagination? I just saw the two of us—me, much younger of course—strolling arm in arm along a river. Just the two of us. We were heading for a restaurant on a pier. The lights were twinkling on the water. You could hear the muffled voices of people having conversations over dinner. Glasses tinkling. Knives and forks. Plates being gathered together. Laughter from the kitchen. We were both very hungry, and we began to run toward the delicious smells. We both started running at the very same time. Without a word between us. Isn't that funny? The imagination.

End Fourth Visit

INTERVIEWER SOLO

INT.: [*To audience.*] The first search I made for my father, I was twelve years old. I had nothing to go on. No picture. No face. Only his name, and the story I'd heard by the fisherman. At first, I had the feeling I would bump into him almost by accident. That somehow, we would recognize each other and meet, as if by magic. My grandmother believed in miracles. She was the only one. She held many superstitions. Most of them connected to the river. If the water rose and the spring peepers began their song before the first day of March, it was a good sign to her. A strong sign. If the water darkened at midday and became flat and glassy, she began to worry. This was a sign of evil. No one was allowed out of the house on a day like this. She told me I would find my father on a street corner, reading a paper, under the crescent moon. She told me the name of the street, the time of night, and even the clothes he'd be wearing. She told me to walk right up to him and kiss him lightly on the shoulder. He would know by the kiss, she said.

Fifth Visit

INT.: One thing I find difficult to believe—

O.M.: Only one?

INT.: Well, yes. For the most part I trust that you're telling me the truth.

O.M.: Why? Why do you trust me? You don't even know me.

INT.: I want to believe you, I guess.

O.M.: But why? You work for the paper.

INT.: I don't know. I like you, for some reason. I don't know why. I feel that you're a kind person. Basically kind.

O.M.: So what is this one thing you don't believe?

INT.: I find it very difficult to believe you could have mistaken someone for your cousin, after knowing him your whole life, tracking him all this time, halfway around the world. How is that possible? Didn't you see his face?

O.M.: No. Of course not.

INT.: What do you mean?

O.M.: Have you ever hunted an animal?

INT.: No. I'm a vegetarian. I've told you.

O.M.: Yes, I forgot. I make a wonderful goulash without meat. Artichoke, mushroom and wine sauce.

INT.: We were talking about hunting—

O.M.: Yes. Every good hunter knows you must never look your prey in the eyes. You must avoid the eyes at all cost.

INT.: Why is that?

O.M.: The eyes transmit fear.

INT.: But an animal can smell and hear.

o.m.: Yes. You must avoid that too, but not with humans. Humans are less sensitive. Dull. The eyes, however, are the same in all species. You must never make contact with the eyes if you intend to kill.

int.: So you never looked into this man's face, or your cousin's?

o.m.: No. Once we left school and went our separate ways he became a form, a shape. He would change clothes, addresses, names, passports. He would gain weight and lose it. He would walk with a limp, run funny, change his stride, his shoes. He tried many things to elude me.

int.: But you always knew who he was? Or—thought you knew?

o.m.: Yes. I had an instinct about him. As though I were living partly inside him. Under his skin.

int.: Until this last time. When you made the mistake.

o.m.: Yes. I underestimated his cleverness. I had lost him for a while in Tuscany. It was several months that I had no clue what had become of him, until one afternoon I overheard a conversation with an innkeeper who was bragging how every month he received an order from a gentleman in New Orleans for a case of Brunello di Montalcino.

int.: That's a wine?

o.m.: Yes. A red. Aged in oak for a minimum of five years. Difficult to find in America. But this particular brand happened to be Carl's favorite. He'd been drinking it for years. Always with dinner and occasionally at lunch. He drank nothing else.

int.: That was your only clue?

o.m.: No. The innkeeper went on to say that this same gentleman had stayed there in Tuscany for a while and used to
come by every day for his glass of Brunello. Regular as clock-
work. I knew it had to be Carl because that inn was where
I'd last seen him.

int.: So, you went straight to New Orleans?

o.m.: Yes. I could hardly wait. The smells in the French Quarter!
The shrimp! The aromas of chicory and Crawfish Étouffée.
I spent a week just roaming the streets with no thoughts
about Carl. I allowed myself to be carried from place to
place by my nose alone. I ate myself silly. I ate until the
pains were so excruciating I could barely walk. I would
struggle down to the Mississippi and sit on a bench gasping
for breath. I would just sit there in a stupor, staring at the
lights of riverboats as they floated by and wait for the pains
to subside.

int.: How did you finally locate Carl?

o.m.: I knew his taste in food. His style of restaurant. There
must be white linen tablecloths. Well-lit, because he always
liked to read while he was eating. A window, facing the street.
And small occupancy, never more than thirty. Seafood was
his favorite but occasionally steak and, always, his bottle of
wine. It wasn't hard to track down which restaurant carried
his wine.

int.: So, once you found him, what did you do?

o.m.: I got a job in the kitchen.

int.: Of this same restaurant?

O.M.: Yes. I prepared salads and pastry at first, then worked my way up.

INT.: You became the cook?

O.M.: Head chef, yes.

INT.: How long did that take you?

O.M.: Several months.

INT.: And Carl continued to frequent the restaurant?

O.M.: Oh, yes. Once he settled on a place he became habitual. Besides, he felt very safe there. He was sure he'd lost me. He had a job right across the street playing piano with a Dixieland band. It was ideal for him.

INT.: And you were absolutely sure it was Carl you'd found?

O.M.: Absolutely. There was no question. It was Carl.

INT.: I still don't understand how you could have got him mixed up with somebody else.

O.M.: I had decided it had to be him. I'd made up my mind. I wanted this thing to be over. Any slight doubts I had, I cast aside. I became excited about finally finishing this long ordeal. It would mean I could then be free. I had decided it must be him.

INT.: So, you watched him die?

O.M.: Yes, I did. I watched him from the kitchen. I cooked him my finest meal. The very finest. My Quail with Pear Amaretto

Sauce. He ate it with total innocence, with no hint of it being his last meal on earth. He left me a large tip, which I still have. I will never spend it until I return to Ameda.

INT.: But now you never will.

O.M.: What?

INT.: Return.

End Fifth Visit

OLD MAN SOLO

O.M.: [*To audience.*] Sometimes, everything falls away and I'm just sitting here in the dark. Just sitting. No thoughts. No sounds. Just sitting. Empty. Like a tree or a stone. But it doesn't last. Things come back to haunt me. Things I don't even recognize. Like demons. Faces. Voices I've never heard before. Places I've never seen. They fill me, then leave again. Just sitting. As though I were never born. As though—I will never die. Other times, I recognize everything. It's all familiar. I remember the village burning. That I do remember. The waves of fire. Waves of screaming. Hot wind. Roaring wind. The faces of my people. All running. These things I'm sure took place. They've left their trace on me.

INTERVIEWER SONG

INT.: [*Singing.*]

Go down, you bloodred roses
Go down.
Oh, you pinks and posies

> Go down, you bloodred roses
> Go down.
>
> It's mighty windy 'round Cape Horn.
>
> Go down, you bloodred roses
> Go down.
> Oh, you pinks and posies
> Go down, you bloodred roses
> Go down.

Sixth Visit

INT.: [*Upstage right, no longer carrying notebook.*] Did you sleep at all?

O.M.: [*Sitting in chair, exhausted and impatient.*] No.

INT.: So the pillows didn't help? The blanket?

O.M.: I laid on the floor.

INT.: Why?

O.M.: I thought the discomfort would cause fatigue.

INT.: Were you trying to punish yourself?

O.M.: No, of course not. For what?

INT.: For sins you may have committed?

O.M.: Sins?

INT.: Yes.

O.M.: What is it you're looking for in me? Why do you keep coming back with these questions?

INT.: [*Moving in.*] I'm drawn to the past.

O.M.: Your father?

INT.: Yes. And you.

O.M.: We have nothing in common. Your father and me.

INT.: I'm not so sure.

O.M.: [*Confrontational.*] I am from the village of Ameda. The weather there is perfect. The soil is perfect. The sky is crystal clear.

INT.: [*She remains elusive and turns to face window upstage.*] Yes, you've told me.

O.M.: I'm very tired. [*Rises and crosses to her.*] I'd like to be left alone now. [*She refuses to turn toward him.*]

INT.: But you can't sleep. You might as well talk to me.

O.M.: Why do you keep persisting in this? How did you find out I was here in the first place?

INT.: I read about it in the papers.

O.M.: The papers always lie. There's no truth in the papers.

INT.: It was no lie that you killed someone.

o.m.: I never saw him actually dead! I saw him gasping for air. Clutching at the tablecloth. Crashing to the floor with his eyes wide open. But never actually dead!

int.: [*Turns, moving to his area downstage of bed for the first time.*] So, now you've changed your story?

o.m.: [*Wildly turning.*] There is no story! I've told you that.

int.: So you think there might be a chance he's still alive?

o.m.: How should I know! I've been arrested, but I never saw the corpse.

int.: [*Stops.*] I have. [*Stands and freezes.*]

[*Pause.*]

o.m.: What?

int.: I saw the body.

o.m.: How? You went and looked at it?

int.: Yes.

o.m.: Where? I don't believe it. Why would you do something like that? Who are you, anyway?

int.: [*Moving closer to him.*] I have a special interest in this. Seeing this through. I was there when they took the ring off his finger. The blue ring.

o.m.: You're making this up! You heard me mention the ring before.

INT.: I was there when they closed his eyes.

O.M.: If you're trying to get a confession out of me, I've already confessed. I'm guilty whether he's alive or dead, so it makes no difference.

INT.: It makes a difference to me.

O.M.: [*Shouts.*] I would like you to leave now.

INT.: Nothing's going to happen to you.

O.M.: Everything is happening to me! I've been arrested! I can't sleep! And now you. You could be here to—

INT.: I thought you didn't care.

O.M.: I care about that. I care about something like that. I don't want to die like a dog.

INT.: Like Carl, you mean?

O.M.: Carl is not dead!

INT.: Yes, I know. Someone else is. Someone you never knew. A complete stranger.

O.M.: What did he look like? This corpse of yours. We'll see if you're telling the truth. Explain this corpse to me. Give me a full description.

INT.: [*Looking away as she describes the body.*] The soles of his feet were thick and calloused.

O.M.: I never saw the soles of his feet! Explain something else about him. Something visible.

INT.: The flesh on his arms hung loose and gray.

O.M.: I never saw his bare arms!

INT.: His face was puffed out like a baby's.

O.M.: That's not Carl! Carl was lean and haunted. His eyes were sunk deep in his face.

INT.: Of course it wasn't Carl.

O.M.: I mean this man—

INT.: I thought you never saw his face. Never looked in his eyes.

O.M.: But this man, whoever he was, looked identical to Carl. Absolutely identical.

INT.: But if you never saw his face—

O.M.: I thought he was Carl! Carl was simply an idea to me by then. I convinced myself it was him.

INT.: An idea?

O.M.: Yes. What color was his hair? Answer me that.

INT.: I can't remember.

O.M.: You see! You're making this whole thing up. You're like all the rest of the press. Fabricate anything just to sell a story. It's shameless! Make a story out of nothing!

INT.: I was there when they opened his mouth and removed his dentures. They set his teeth on a stainless-steel table and attached a yellow tag with wire to them. The tag had numbers on it written in black. The numbers were the date and the time of death. They attached another tag with the same numbers to the big toe of his right foot. Then they wheeled the body away. The yellow tag on his toe fluttered slightly like a tiny flag, then disappeared through two swinging doors. The doors kept flapping for a while, then stopped. His teeth were left behind on the stainless-steel table. The gums were synthetic pink and there was still a piece of salad caught between the molars. I turned the yellow tag over and on the other side were more black numbers. His date of birth.

End Sixth Visit

OLD MAN SOLO

o.m.: [*To audience.*] One night, I was walking. I remember this. I was walking on the streets. Somewhere. I don't know which town. I don't know which country. I had no destination. Just walking. I remember I stopped. I stopped on a corner and waited for something. Just waiting. I had no idea what I was waiting for. Suddenly, I felt someone touch my shoulder. A hand. I turned. And there was Carl. He was very close. I could have touched his face, he was so close. And then he turned and disappeared. I'm sure it was him. I'm sure it was Carl.

INTERVIEWER SOLO

int.: [*To audience.*] One night, everything was exactly like my grandmother told me. All the signs were there at once. I saw

him. I know it was him. Sitting on a bench. I saw him lick
his thumb and turn the front page of the *Picayune*. His back
was to me but he was wearing the blue ring she'd told me
about. The moon was just like she said. Still. Absolutely still.
Just hung there like a white knife. I could barely breathe.
The air was so thick. Sweat dripped from the back of his
neck. I couldn't move. For a long time I couldn't move toward
him. I kept seeing the kiss in my mind. What it would be
like. The smell of his shirt. The kiss. I couldn't move.

Seventh Visit

[*Old Man upstage center, staring out window, lost in thought.*]

INT.: What do you do when I'm not here?

O.M.: [*Surprised.*] I like the window.

INT.: What do you see?

O.M.: [*Disturbed and speaking in abrupt short phrases.*] This
morning there was a woman with luggage. Heavy bags in
each hand. She seemed to be moving out of her house. She
spent a long time locking her door with different keys. I
couldn't tell if she was searching for the right key or if
maybe there were several locks. She seemed reluctant to
leave her doorstep. [*Gestures toward window.*] She kept looking up high at a window, as though she were waiting for
someone to appear. Then she'd turn and stare at the street.
Do you suppose everyone secretly carries that feeling?

INT.: What feeling?

O.M.: That there might be some companion. Some invisible partner. [*Pause.*]

INT.: [*Quietly.*] Are you calmer now?

O.M.: From when?

INT.: My last visit. You seemed very excited.

O.M.: [*Crossing to bed.*] I can't remember.

INT.: Did you get any sleep?

O.M.: [*Seated facing downstage.*] Last night—

INT.: Yes?

O.M.: Last night, while I was waiting for sleep, I began to imagine all sorts of things.

INT.: Like what?

O.M.: I began to imagine—

INT.: What?

O.M.: That you were somehow, through some cruel coincidence, the daughter of this man.

INT.: Which man?

O.M.: The murdered man! The man I accidentally killed.

INT.: [*Turns toward the window and stares out window during the following dialogue.*] And what else did you imagine?

O.M.: That your only purpose for being here was revenge.

INT.: I see.

O.M.: It's ridiculous, isn't it?

INT.: You're the one who imagined it.

O.M.: Yes, but you're not, are you?

INT.: What?

O.M.: The daughter of this man!

INT.: What if I was?

O.M.: But you couldn't be. You would have taken action by now. Why would you wait?

INT.: [*Turns around to face him.*] Why did you wait for Carl?

O.M.: I've told you already. It was my whole life. [*Tries to get up, fails, sits.*] It was the very reason I was born.

INT.: [*Slowly moving away.*] What else did you imagine?

O.M.: I saw birds.

INT.: Birds?

O.M.: Yes. In my mind. Amazing birds. All colors. [*Rises.*] Flying. The air was thick with them. All different kinds. Species. Birds that didn't belong together.

INT.: Why birds?

O.M.: They're not stuck to this earth. Not stuck, but flying. [*A burst of energy*.] I was thinking I wanted to sing. Some song or other, but for some reason I couldn't think of one. Imagine that. All the songs I've ever heard in my life and I couldn't think of one. And there were all these birds just singing, without thinking. Just—singing. [*Makes noises and gestures suggesting birds singing and flying.*]

INT.: Would you like to sing now?

O.M.: I can't think of one. I still can't.

INT.: There must be something from your childhood.

O.M.: You're not here to finish me, are you? You wouldn't have come just for that.

INT.: Let me help you think of one.

O.M.: You're not just waiting for the right moment to stab me in the chest?

INT.: Don't be afraid.

O.M.: Will you give me some warning? Some sign?

INT.: [*Singing and moving downstage, facing audience.*] "Three old crows, sitting on a fence. Caw, caw, caw." You remember that one?

O.M.: I never was a child.

INT.: [*Singing.*] "Three old crows, sitting on a fence. Fiddle, McGhee, McGaw."

O.M.: I am from the village of Ameda. The soil there is perfect. The sky is perfect. The water is sweet and clear. There was never any need for singing.

End Seventh Visit

INTERVIEWER SOLO

INT.: [*To audience.*] A suspicion. It will grow now. By itself. Vengeance doesn't interest me. A father I never knew. A corpse. A kiss that never took place. I was born by the river. Close to the river. Even as a baby, I could feel the pull of the green water.

Eighth Visit

[*Interviewer enters with a frying pan, vegetables, mangoes, almonds, oil, spices, etc.; also a small electric hot plate, two dishes, knives, forks, napkins, whatever's necessary for the Old Man to cook. She sets everything down on a small table.*]

O.M.: What have you brought now?

INT.: They've given me permission to let you cook. They were very nice about it.

O.M.: I've told you—I'm not interested in food now. I have no desire to cook. Why do you keep persisting in this?

INT.: I found ripe mangoes. And almonds. I've got everything here.

O.M.: Why you? Why you at this late date? It's impossible. Why couldn't I have met you long before?

INT.: I wasn't there. I wasn't born.

O.M.: I suppose—love is out of the question.

INT.: I've brought all the ingredients.

O.M.: I don't see brown sugar.

INT.: Yes, I've got that too. Right here!

O.M.: I don't see fennel—the "symbol of flattery." The "emblem of heroism." Did you know that?

INT.: No. I had no idea. But it's here. I have it right here. I know I brought it. [*Searches through the herbs.*]

O.M.: Marjoram? The "joy of the mountain."

INT.: Yes!

O.M.: And the feathery anise? The carrot family. From Egypt and Greece.

INT.: Of course. Yes, I have that. I know I bought anise.

O.M.: Cardamom? The "sense of well-being." Tarragon? "Pure bliss. Seductive, unselfish sharing."

INT.: Yes.

o.m.: And the bay? "Glory. Wisdom and glory. I change but in death."

int.: I have it all.

o.m.: Did you know that Caesar—Julius Caesar—wore the bay leaf to disguise his baldness?

int.: No. No, I didn't.

o.m.: Isn't that strange? How could a leaf even remotely resemble human hair?

int.: I don't know. [*Pause.*]

o.m.: Didn't you tell me that you liked me? Yesterday or the day before? That you thought I might be a kind person? Basically kind.

int.: Yes. Yes, I did.

o.m.: I'm so lucky to have met you. At this late date. If I cook— if I cook for you—this one last meal—this Chutney with Mangoes and Almonds—this food from heaven, as you say—

int.: Yes.

o.m.: If I make this one last dish and set it before you and watch you savor every mouthful—

int.: I will. I know I will.

o.m.: Will you then promise—will you make me a solemn oath that you'll never come back and plague me with your constant questions? Never again.

INT.: Yes. I promise.

O.M.: You won't change your mind in the middle of the night? Sit bolt upright in your bed with one last burning question?

INT.: No, I won't.

O.M.: How can you be sure? How can you be absolutely sure you've gotten to the bottom of this?

INT.: I can't. But I promise I won't come back.

O.M.: No. You must come back. It's just the questions. No more questions. Well, I won't be here anyway. This is my last day.

INT.: I'll miss you.

O.M.: Yes. We've gotten to know each other a little.

INT.: Yes.

O.M.: Impossible almost.

INT.: What?

O.M.: That I would know one more person, before my death. And someone—like you. Carl was my last friend on earth.

INT.: Would you like me to try to find him for you?

O.M.: No. What would I say? There's nothing more to say now. It's finished.

INT.: He might have something to say to you.

O.M.: No. It's done. It's finished. Too much time has passed.

INT.: He might be willing to start over.

O.M.: No. I could never begin again. I have no desire. Only a growing sense of overwhelming fatigue.

INT.: Do you have the strength to cook?

O.M.: For you, I do. You must help me, though.

INT.: Yes. What can I do?

O.M.: You must prepare the pan. The oil.

INT.: Good. They were kind enough to loan us a hot plate. They say they've allowed this to happen before in special cases. A last meal. [*She plugs in the hot plate and begins to prepare the frying pan.*]

O.M.: The temperature must be perfect. A single drop of clear water will give you the hint. Just before the steam arises, a drop of oil. Pure saffron. In the very center of the skillet. Not to the side. Not anywhere near the edge.

INT.: Yes. [*She follows his instructions carefully as he moves toward the other ingredients and begins to peel the mango.*]

O.M.: The temperature is the entire foundation for everything else to follow. If it's off by even a fraction, disaster will surely come in its wake.

INT.: I'll watch it closely.

o.m.: The meat of the mango must be exposed slowly to the surrounding air. The skin cannot be ripped away as you would with an orange. Exploding into the light. The juice popping into your face and eyes. The mango is much softer. Much gentler by nature.

int.: Yes. Such an incredible smell!

o.m.: It needs coaxing. Great care must be taken to separate it from its original hide. The use of the fingers must be guarded to ward off any undue bruising of the flesh. [*Continuing to peel the mango.*] Panic has no place in this. The fingers must caress the fruit. They must exude a kindness. A kindness that matches the gift of the fruit itself. A loving respect toward the origin of this meeting. This touching. This joining of my ancient hunger and the food that feeds it. This golden fruit from heaven. Now. Now, I am a cook. Now, finally, I am only a cook.

End Eighth Visit

OLD MAN SOLO

[*Old Man rises in dark and comes forward into a pool of light center stage.*]

o.m.: [*To audience.*] Many years ago, when the world was new, my great-great-great-great grandfather was plowing an open field with his mule, when the sky closed in above him. The air turned black as night, then shattered into a brilliant green and yellow light. There before him lay my grandfather's mule. Then the killings began. They have never stopped. This is the story they told me. What else could I believe. [*During the solo the Interviewer appears upstage left and sings with her back to the audience.*]

INT.: [*Singing.*]

> Go down, you bloodred roses
> Go down.
> Oh, you pinks and posies
> Go down, you bloodred roses
> Go down.

[*At the end of singing, and after Old Man concludes his speech, she removes a scarf from her head and waves it in the air as Old Man did in First Visit.*]